Apollo 20. The Disclosure

LUCA SCANTAMBURLO

Apollo 20 The Disclosure

Lulu.com

Lulu Press, Inc. - Lulu Enterprises, Inc.

FIRST EDITION

Apollo 20. The Disclosure

Lulu.com,
Lulu Press, Inc. - Lulu Enterprises, Inc., USA
First Edition, January 2010

USA, 2010, ISBN 978-1-4452-7397-6

  Front Cover: an illustration – by the Author's fantasy – of a LM landing on the moon. © L. Scantamburlo, 2010. Jacket design by the Author. On the back cover, elaborated frames from Apollo 20 and 19 footage, with the permission of "retiredafb" and "moonwalker1966delta".

2008

<<[...] the UFO phenomenon is real [...] It's been well covered up by all our governments for the last 60 years [...] yes, we have been visited..>>

Dr. Edgar MITCHELL

former NASA astronaut (Apollo 14 LMP and retired Navy Captain) interviewed on the phone by *Kerrang!Radio*, host Nick Margerrison (*The Night Before*), U.K., July 2008

1996

<<Somewhere at some level in our Government [...] someone has made a decision to allow me [...] and a few others [...] to continue to do this, because we are doing in a no threatening in a no frighting kind of way.>>

Robert O. DEAN

retired U.S. Army Sergeant Major, in an interview granted in 1996 to a Britisher (source: UFOVISION's video)

1987

<<[...] I occasionally think how quickly our differences worldwide would vanish if we were facing an alien threat from outside this world. And yet, I ask you, is not an alien force already among us? >>

U.S. President Ronald REAGAN

September 21, 1987, 42d Session of the U. N. General Assembly in New York.

INTRODUCTION

I can't begin the introduction of this book without thanking my close friends, my family, all the people from several countries of the world who have helped me to understand some aspects of this controversial case: the Apollo 19 and 20 story. Many individuals wrote me and they have been still writing me since 2007. Some of them gave me help behind the scenes - as anonymous sources - pointing out small details of Space exploration and Space history, not well-known, which can corroborate some parts of this outstanding story.

A story that contains some misleading data, video fakes and contradictory information, and this is an important thing to say and to remember. Three of my main sources of information and discussion are an engineer from South America (Mr. G.) and two North Americans: Mr. W., and another American citizen who is founder of *SpaceHeroes.org*, a website which tried to investigate the case in public and present opinions and data not discussed properly. Often criticized, we should remember what its link „about" said:

<<*SpaceHeroes.org is dedicated to investigating spectacular feats of daring in space and identifying/honoring Space Heroes — men and women involved in space missions meeting all the requirements under 14 CFR 1221.2 but whose missions were so dangerous (and potentially socially and economically disruptive if disclosed) that such activities may have been kept secret from the general public.*>>[A]

Another source of information and discussion will be disclosed for the first time in this text: he is a well-known retired American pilot, former captain for US Airline and pilot for several Aircraft Corporations. He has also flown operations for the CIA. Others individuals have come forward with their names and surnames, giving me written permissions to quote their comments or just them as source of information.

Paolo Rosati - an Italian citizen who is a fond of Space history and an indipendent scholar during his free time - is one of them. Another one is the Israeli citizen Haim Ram Bar Ilan, nicknamed „Rami", who is an artist, a designer and a Yom-Kippur War veteran. Rami has become a pen friend of mine, and - published on this pages - you can see part of

---

A   http://www.spaceheroes.org/about.html; it seems that the website is not available anymore on-line; maybe the owner did not renew the hosting of the website.

his artistic work on the Apollo 20 case. I have dedicated a tribute page for him, to whom it may concern (see Appendix V).

But also reserarchers, (I can mention dr. V.M.M., a Serbian scientist), engineers, and other journalists have showed interest. Some of them have contributed to open the debate publicly. In Canada Dirk Vander Ploeg, while for USA I can mention Kevin Smith, Bob Kiviat, Don Allis, the British Bill Ryan (busy with Kerry Cassidy in their Project Camelot), and especially the radio host Zen Garcia (Georgia, USA).

For Italy I remember Maurizio Baiata, Pablo Ayo, and the radio host Stefano Famà with Salvatore Giusa.

Moreover, Sabrina Pieragostini (from the television news *StudioAperto* of *Italia 1* TV channel, a network beloging to the Italian company Mediaset) is the journalist who has finally brought the case – with its lights and shadows - to the attention of the big media, in a report-interview with me for a special episode of the television programme named *Mistero*[1] presented by Enrico Ruggeri and broadcasted on October 25, 2009.

Their efforts have balanced the presence of a sort of disinformation campaign that has tried not only to emphasize actual contradictions, but to destroy the entire probable disclosure, spreading false information on me, on the story itself, and creating false videos uploaded on YouTube to deceive the general public.

Officially cancelled by NASA because of budget reasons, Apollo 19 and Apollo 20 manned space missions (and for someone even Apollo 18) would have rescheduled as classified military space missions involving not only the United States of America, but also the former Soviet Union, with the targets to investigate some lunar anomalies found out on the far side of the Moon, independently by Soviets before, and Americans later on.

Among the identified lunar anomalies: a huge cigar-shaped object, two triangular objects, and ruins of an ancient base. All of them would be of alien origin.

The Apollo 20 crew would have been composed by William Rutledge (Commander), Leona Marietta Snyder, and Alexei Leonov (the famous Soviet cosmonaut and Hero of Soviet Union).

---

1   <<*Gli alieni fra noi: i dossier segreti*>>, programme by Studio Aperto and Mistero, Italia 1, Italian network of Mediaset, broadcasted on October 25, 2009.

Therefore these Apollo 19 and 20 - joint US and USSR operations - would have been DoD missions (Department of Defense missions, mainly USAF missions in this case), with NASA assistance and collaboration of the Soviets (Yevpatoria would have been one of the mission controls from where Alexei Leonov could take orders, but the main Mission Control would have located in USA, in the famous Vandenberg Air Force Base).

The ASTP (Apollo Soyuz Test Project) – occurred in July 1975 – was <<*the honeymoon before a moon landing mission, it was presented as a simple "shaking hands " mission in 1975*>>, William Rutledge explained in my written interview with him, taken place at the end of May 2007 and carried out by my YouTube Account/General Messages.

According to this first whistleblower of the case – by the nickname of „retiredafb" on YouTube and a.k.a. William Rutledge - Apollo 20 would have been launched with a Saturn V from the Vandenberg AFB, on August 16, 1976.

According to the second whistleblower of the story - „moonwaklker1966delta" on YouTube – the other secret space mission Apollo 19 would have always been launched with another Saturn rocket, from the same base (Vandenberg AFB in California), but on February 2nd, 1976: so just a few months before Apollo 20, which was the following secret manned lunar mission launched towards the backside of the Moon because of the failure of Apollo 19.

It seems that Apollo 19 failed because of a sudden incident in Space, at the end of TLI manoeuvre: this was told by William Rutledge himself at the end of May 2007, and later confirmed and corrected by „moonwalker1966delta", the alleged Apollo 19 Commander (CMDR). As the matter of fact, the Apollo 19 Commander told me they survived after the incident in Space, and they did not die. Why did William Rutledge tell me the Apollo 19 crew was lost? And what about the classified missions and the lunar anomalies? Did they tell us the truth, or just kernels of truth?

To help the reader of this book, in its first part – besides new writings both as foot-notes and new main text considerations - I will present my two interviews and almost all my articles that I have written about the topic in English language, for my website *www.angelismarriti.it*: since the first interview with the Apollo 20 Commander („retiredafb") - an interview that, by the way, has been spontaneously translated by internauts from English into many languages - to the second very important interview with the alleged Apollo 19 Commander (the insider known as „moonwalker1966delta" on YouTube).

The second part of the book contains studies, unpublished information, and other my considerations which can help to have an open-minded point of view, as much as possible.

This choice – in my opinion – should help the reader to realize my way as former reporter and journalist. The chronological order of my Web articles and interviews here presented, will show my personal understanding of the case, my mistakes and difficulties, and above all my growing awareness of the importance of this controversial disclosure for all mankind.

The general public – and you as reader – will be the judge of this story. Virgilio – the ancient Latin poet – wrote in the past

,, *Carpent tua poma nepotes*"[2].

These words were chosen for the Apollo 20 mission patch.

Perhaps we are those grandchildren.

Luca Scantamburlo

Italy, December 2009

---

2   From *Bucoliche* by Virgilio, IX, 50. <<*I frutti [degli alberti che tu innesi] li coglieranno i nipoti*>> says the Italian translation from Latin by Servio Marzio, *Cum Grano Salis. Il latino per l'uomo di mondo*, pag. 32, a small handbook published in Italy by A Vallardi, Garzanti Editore, 1992. This poetic line means that the grandchildren will pick the fruits (of the trees you graft). It is an expression used in modern times to indicate hope for the future, but it also means that mankind works for future generations.

PART I

MY INTERVIEWS AND REPORTS

With respect to my original interviews and reports published on the Web - and here presented on paper – sometimes the text has been corrected where there were evident grammatical mistakes, and integrated with some new foot-notes, but for example "retiredafb"'s syntax and his not clear form have not been changed.

The original links on-line and mentioned in the reports, were active at the time and of course I am not responsible of any change or removal. In the book text I have omitted some of them, where not necessary for the comprehension (a few of them were related to photos here not reproduceable because they are copyrighted material, or that I have decided not reproduce). So, in some Web articles of mine I have removed the original references to figures, images and captions.

Moreover, most of the videos (and comments) posted by "retiredafb" on YouTube, have been removed by "retiredafb" himself, that's why original links do not work anymore. Fortunately I saved his texts before disappeared. Through them – not available on Internet anymore – and through my correspondence with him, we can understand better this astonishing testimony, and the following one provided by „moonwalker1966delta", the alleged Apollo 19 Commander.

CHAPTER I

An Alien Spaceship On the Moon: Interview with William Rutledge, Member of the Apollo 20 Crew

Written interview with William Rutledge, an Apollo 20 astronaut (1976). Interview carried out by my YouTube Account/General Messages.[3]

A secret joint space mission on the Moon, result of an American-Soviet collaboration taken place in August 1976? Is it possible? Why not, if you consider that the existence of a Federal Agency like NRO (National Reconnaissance Office), and its missions of overhead reconnaissance, "were declassified in September 1992" (according to its official website). And is it really possible that such a collaboration has been prepared to explore a huge alien spaceship found on the backside of the Moon?

William Rutledge (according to his story, a man of 76 years old who lives in Rwanda, former of Bell Laboratories and employed by USAF) is the name of the "deep throat" who, since April 2007, has been disclosing information and spreading a lot of video and photographic material on YouTube, about the presumed Apollo 20 space mission. His user name on YouTube is "retiredafb", and the most amazing footage he released so far is the presumed flyover of an ancient alien spaceship found on the backside of the Moon by the Apollo 15 crew.

The last official space mission to the Moon with crew was the Apollo 17 (NASA), which took place in December 1972, and the Apollo 20

---

3 UPDATING

I have decided it is better avoiding to name the people who work for NASA now and mentioned by W. Rutledge in the answer nr.24, because it is necessary, in spite of his amazing video footages and his detailed report, waiting for further evidence about this amazing story, which is showing some contradictory aspects. As fact, in spite of their names are true and in public domain as Governmental employees, so far they are not known as historical leading characters, and there is no proof of a previous contact with W. Rutledge - But the things could change... Let's see what happens.

L.S.

June 30, 2007

mission was cancelled by NASA in January 1970. But the presumed footage of Apollo 20 is not the only material which came out in the last weeks: it was also released by William Rutledge a presumed studio for the flyover of the assumed alien spaceship (available on YouTube as the so-called preflight study for Apollo 20). And moreover on YouTube we have also several shots of the strange object on the backside of the Moon (whose numbers would be AS20-1020, AS20-1022 and AS20-FWD-7250). According to the YouTube file-card on William Rutledge, who uploaded the controversial footages and shots,

<<*Apollo 20 went to the moon august 16 1976. Destination was Iszak D, southwest of Delporte Crater, farside of the moon. The mission was soviet-american. Crew was William Rutledge CDR, former of bell laboratories, leona snyder CSP bell laboratories, and alexei leonov, soviet cosmonaut former "apollo soyouz" (mission one year earlier).*>>

There are a few inconsistencies in William Rutledge's memories that you can find in reading this interview. It could be comprehensible if you think about an old man (76 years old) who is trying to recall historical facts and events of his life. So, I am not astonished if Rutledge, for instance in talking about the former Russian President Boris Yeltsin who used tanks and troops during the assault to the Parliament building, recalled the years 1995 or 1994 when the exact year of the small civil war was 1993 (<<*[...] I went to the Ural in 1995 or 1994, can't recall, responding to an invitation, but it was a mess here, I crossed Moscow when tanks were shooting the Russian parliament*>> by W. Rutledge, from the answer nr.8 of the interview).

I have verified it later on an encyclopaedia, but I could not answer before to such a question. I remembered only it occurred at the beginning of the '90s.

On the other hand William Rutledge showed me a knowledge of Geology, Chemistry and of space exploration history, using specific terms. For example, he mentioned in the interview a not well-know term: the "feldspathoid", a "mineral consisting of an aluminous silicate that has too little silica to form feldspar" (*Webster's Third New International Dictionary*, Könemann, 1993, pag. 835).

So, I have good grounds for believing William Rutledge's testimony: first of all there really is (was?) a strange and big object on the far side of the Moon, and its shape is very close to that one showed in the video on YouTube: I am talking about the object visible in a couple of NASA pictures taken by the Apollo 15 mission. The cigar-shaped object looks like leant beside a crater, lightly oblique; and the visible zone in the footage is very similar to the visible region in some originals NASA photos taken by Apollo 15: the Moon region coordinates where there is the unusual object are the following: Latitude: 10° S - Longitude: 117.5° E, Southwest of Delporte and North of Izsak. I have checked on a Lunar chart: it is on the backside of the Moon.

The official NASA photos are available on the website of the Lunar and Planetary Institute (LPI, in Houston), which is a "research institute that provides support services to NASA and the planetary science community": the links to find the pictures (the AS15-P-9630 and the AS15-P-9625, from the the Apollo Image Atlas) are the following:

http://www.lpi.usra.edu/resources/apollo/frame/?AS15-P-9625

http://www.lpi.usra.edu/resources/apollo/frame/?AS15-P-9630

Moreover, it is meaningful that the links were provided by William Rutledge (how did he know the details of those panoramic picture?).

A second reason, in my opinion, is that William Rutledge is not gaining money from doing that. A third reason is the detailed story he told me in the following interview, full of technical and other specific aspects coherent among them. There are just some incomplete biographical notes about the famous NASA astronauts. But he answered kindly to every single question I have put to him, without hesitation, and he provided several names of the presumed American and Soviet people involved in that classified space mission. Some of them are still alive. It could be interesting to be able having a comment from them.

The fourth reason is the quality of the footages on YouTube, which seem consistent with a shot equipment available during the '70s and the first '80s. I have asked to an expert in shot, an Italian friend of mine whose name initials are F.D. His comment about the footage spread by William Rutledge was the following:

<<[...] i punti luce sovraesposti e la relativa 'scia' presentano tutte le caratteristiche dei difetti delle telecamere basate su tubo di tipo VIDICON. La 'scia' consiste in una persistenza del segnale video all'interno del tubo. [...] Nonostante quest'ultimo sia un sistema di ripresa televisivo obsoleto, oggi la ditta Hamamatsu (www.hamamatsu.com) realizza telecamere VIDICON all'infrarosso.>>

In English it means: <<[...] the overexposed light points and the relative trail show all the features of the TV cameras faults based on VIDICON-type tube. The 'trail' is composed of a persistence of the video signal inside the tube. [...] In spite this one is an obsolete TV shot system, today the Hamamatsu firm (www.hamamatsu.com) makes infrared VIDICON cameras.>>

And, as a matter of fact, among the several different varieties of photographic equipment aboard the Apollo 17, there was a Westinghouse color TV camera, which could used in the command module, handheld or bracket-mounted. It is almost obvious thinking to a similar camera equipment for the presumed Apollo 20, taken place in 1976 according to William Rutledge.

(source:http://www.lpi.usra.edu/expmoon/Apollo17/A17_Photography_cameras.html.)

In any case, the public will be the first judge of this story, which could become in the near future the definitive proof that we are not alone in the Universe.

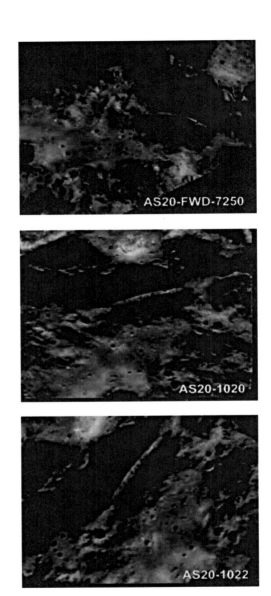

Snapshots from the video <<*ALIEN SPACESHIP ON THE MOON stills from APOLLO 20*>>
posted on May 3, 2007, on YouTube, by "retiredafb"; see Appendix II;
reproduction by kind permission of "retiredafb" (William Rutledge)

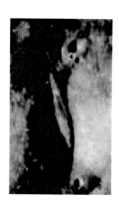

Details from official NASA panoramic photos, but rotated of 90 °: from AS15-P-9625 on the left, and from AS15-P-9630 on the right; Mission Apollo 15, 1971,

Latitude / Longitude: 19° S / 117.5° E, Camera Altitude: 117 km; far side of the Moon;

Image and data credit: The Lunar and Planetary Institute – NASA Photos

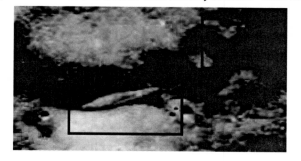

Above, another detail of AS15-P-9625, with my markings on the presumed lunar anomalies pointed out by "retiredafb" and "moonwalker1966delta".

Foreword for the readers

In the following interview granted by William Rutledge who lives now in Africa, I have corrected (where I could) the orthographical mistakes that there were in the answers (e.g. I have put the right capital letters and the right apostrophes), but I did not change the syntactical construction of the sentences made by William Rutledge. Where I was not able to understand his words, I have put some dots between square brackets.

W. Rutledge told me he is now an old man with some problems to the his articulations; moreover, William explained to me that he's always nervous when he writes. That's why on YouTube you can find some mistakes in his comments (user name: retiredafb) posted with the footages. Anyway, here you are some words written by him for the foreword to the following interview:

> << I don't use English since 1990 but Kinyarwanda and French, and I write quickly, sometimes letters are missing because I'm busy writing the next one, or it is another on the keyboard which is used, but that's a detail...>>

1) Luca Scantamburlo: *First of all I want to thank you for your time and availability. It means a lot for me and, I guess, for all the people around the world, very curious about what it is going on YouTube after the release of your amazing video footages and information on the presumed "Apollo 20" space mission. Now we can begin our interview. Because of my professional activity, I will start from a skeptical point of view. So please, I kindly ask you to understand it. You will have the space to answer and for explaining your reasons.*

What is your name? How old are you and are you an American citizen? Sometimes your written English contains some orthographical mistakes... Are you forgetting your language rules (e.g., you wrote "maicroscope" instead of "microscope")? Somebody on the Web said you do not seem (considering your writings) an American-English native land...

William Rutledge: I'm not offended, I like to answer to skeptics, you cannot imagine what kind of messages I receive. That's my name, William Rutledge, no Standford Rutledge, it's another one. Born in 1930 in Belgium, American citizen, I know about mistakes, I'm writing too fast with arthrose problems and I'm always nervous when I'm writing, it's like trying to contain a flow of water. I'm not accustomed to speak in English anymore since 1990. I have learned Kinyarwanda and use French, sometimes German because Rwanda is a former Belgium-German colony.

2) L.S. *How long have you been living in Rwanda and why did you move overthere?*

W.R. It 's a woman who brought me to Rwanda, maybe I was searching for somebody like one person who shared my life before. Personally speaking, I have always been sensible to Africa born women. (Buzz Aldrin was also sensible, he was the only astronaut participating in a walk after martin Luther King's death, it's not a well known story). I established myself with a new identity in Kigali in 1990, streets have no names here. I stayed in Nyiamirambo quarter till 1994, war pushed me to the north west of the country, near the Congo Kinshasa frontier. Rwandan authorities do not know my past, my friends do.

3) L.S. *Can you tell me anything about your life? Where are you from? Where did you study?*

W.R. I've written on this on my others answers, Avro, Chance Vought, just consider that USAF uses every person who can bring skills, white, black, woman, every citizen. It was different with NASA, all astronauts were West Point students, only Alan Bean was an artist, Armstrong was a philosopher and Aldrin a spiritual man.

4) L.S. *How did you become an astronaut with NASA (I suppose) in the '70s?*

W.R. NASA didn't employ me, USAF did, I had worked on the study of foreign technology, RUSSIAN only, study about the N1[4] project, AJAX plane project and the Mig Foxbat 25. I had some skills for using computer navigation and was a volunteer for the MOL-Gemini project. USAF recalled that, I have been chosen later for Apollo 20 because I was one of the rare pilots who didn't believe in God (it has changed since 1990) but it was a criterion in 1976. It was not the status of the NASA

---

4 N-1 was the powerful rocket developed by Soviets to go to the Moon with a manned space mission, comparable to the US Saturn V, but all the launches failed.

astronauts. Not believing in God made the difference. That's all.

5) L.S. *Can you prove who you are with some photos or documents of yours, taken during the training by NASA or even before, during your work at the Bell Laboratories? Can you send them to me as attachments, for a publication?*

W.R. Yes, I will put them online, but I will focus on Leonov, to end hoax controversy.

6) L.S. *When and above all why did you decide to disclose these information about classified space missions and is there anybody who is protecting you?*

W.R. It's the announcement of "the wonder of it all"[5] maybe, and 2012 is coming fast. I also think that UFOs will appear more often starting from September 2007. A lot of people died around me in Rwanda, and I have more time to take care of this. About protection, please understand it's hard to speak of my armoury.

7) L.S. *After the "Apollo 20" mission, taken place in August 1976 according to the information you have provided, what did you do and when did you leave the U.S.A.?*

W.R. After Apollo 20, several things happened, I was not aware of how the material collected would be used. I thought Space Shuttle was a bad idea, I've worked on the KH 11 project before retiring.

8) L.S. *In your writings provided on YouTube you mentioned the members of the "Apollo 20" crew: among them there is the former Soviet cosmonaut, Alexei Leonov. I remember he is still alive. Does he know what you are doing on the Web? Did you talk with him before April 2007 and if the answer is no, aren't you afraid about what he could do or tell?*

---

5   *The Wonder Of It All,* is a film by Jeffrey Roth about the 12 men who walked on the Moon. I did not realize this at once. At the end of May 2007, when this written interview took place and was spread on Internet, the documentary was not well-known yet in Europe where I live, and I had not any idea about what William Rutledge meant talking about "the wonder of it all". Later on I found out that on April 20-21, 2007, there was an official presentation of the film at the Newport Beach Film Festival in California, with former astronauts John W. Young and Alan Bean as special guests. But when I watched the video trailer for the first time, I could understand a possible connection with the obscure answer given me by William Rutledge, the alleged Apollo 20 CDR. The video trailer, in his written notes, says: <<*Only 12 Men Have Ever Walked On the Moon*>>. Only 12 men? This is what the official Space history tells.

W.R. Leonov is not aware of all this, I cannot contact him, contacts were completely lost in 1982-1984, I went to the Ural in 1995 or 1994, can't recall, responding to an invitation, but it was a mess here, I crossed Moscow when tanks were shooting the Russian parliament. Cant' imagine his reaction. If he discovers the videos without preparation, he can confirm or leave at once. If he is warned, and prepared, he can deny.

9) L.S. *A question about the dialogues subtitles on the "spaceship footage": did you make them or did somebody else make them? There are some mistakes (e.g., the personal pronoun is "I", with the capital letter, not "i" as there is written). What about the original dialogues? Were there in the footage? Did you have problems with the codecs during the transfer?*

W.R. Yes, plenty of problems, subtitles are made just before transfer, I have to work with the distance, I'll be back in Rwanda in July. I asked to put the flyover very quickly, they made the subtitles in one hour, buried instead of burried, aperture to 1.8 is not at the right place, there are mistakes but is does not shock me. The Apollo 11 mention at the beginning of the film surprised me, it is on the original film, one internaut signaled that to me. The films are not the first generation, some of them were copied in 1982 I'm sure of this, some have a blue background from the end of the 70's.

10) L.S. *There are in the dialogues between the astronauts and the Mission Control, some expressions that I do not understand: for instance, "CSM", "DSKY" and "Vandenberg Twenty". I could think that "DSKY" is about the position on the Moon (close to the Izsak crater) and that the "Vandenberg Twenty" is about the Mission Control, located by the Vandeberg Air Force Base, in California. Can you explain them?*

W.R. CSM is Command Service Module, DSKY was the computer "display keyboard", we used many acronyms. AGC is Apollo Guidance Computer, same that DSKY, but located in the Apollo spacecraft and coupled with a telescope ([...] on the LM).

In some videos, the first image you see is the DSKY panel with lines prog indicates the program running verb and noun verb indicates what the DSKY has to do and show. Before filming I had to enter verb 15 (display MET, mission elapsed time, or hours minutes seconds since lift-off, then noun 65 for displaying on there rows, hours on the first line minutes on the second, and seconds/tens of seconds on the third line). Then in every movie we put the date on the beginning of the shot, MET, Mission Elapsed Time, hours since lift-off. In the flyover movie, the computer indicates 144 hours if I remember.

Capcom (CC) is the function of the unique officer charged of transmission to astronauts. He gathers all information and transmit them to the astronauts, news from the ground, instructions for the corrections, wake up calls, three persons relay.

The syntax was "Vandenberg" calling Vandenberg next "twenty" a call from twenty. Inverted when starting from Earth: Capcom- Twenty or sometimes EEcom- Twenty Guido - Twenty when we had a special work to do, docking, correction. When undocking was made the communications were different. Vandenberg Constellation (name of the Apollo spacecraft); Vandenberg Phoenix (name of the LM). The Apollo 19 Apollo spacecraft was Endymion and Artemis was the Lunar Module name.

11) L.S. *I would like to know something more about the preparation of the "Apollo 20" mission. From where and when the Saturn rocket was launched and how many people were involved in that classified mission. Can you do some names?*

W.R. 300 people were involved on the preparation, but more other witnesses in Vandenberg. It was launched from this AFB. More witnesses, yes, many people saw departures in the sky, cameras were forbidden all around the Vandenberg site, but today a lot of Space spotters film every launch of Delta rockets, from towns. Other people saw this launch but not knowing it was a Saturn 5. One internaut viewing the launch video says this launch is a Saturn 1B. If today, with all available information, somebody makes such a mistake, you can image how it was in 1976. The preparation was long, subject of cancellations, new starts. Russians had the first information since 1966, I don't know what was their source.

12) L.S. *Can you tell me anything about the Russian collaboration to "Apollo 20"?*

W.R. James Chipman Fletcher for USA and Valentin Alexeiev for Russia, Werner Von Braun was one of the happy viewer. Capcom were Charles Peter Conrad[6] and James Irwin.

13) L.S. *Tell me something about the "Apollo 18" and the "Apollo 19" missions; specially about the last one and its failure. Was it a classified mission with the same goal of the "Apollo 20"? Tell me about your ex girlfriend, Stephanie Ellis, "first American woman in Space" according to what you wrote to me in a former letter. The official space history does not include her as astronaut...*

W.R. Apollo 18 was the Apollo-Soyuz project, the honeymoon before a moon landing mission, it was presented as a simple "shaking hands " mission in 1975. Apollo 19 and 20 were hazardous missions. On long duration flight the helium pressure was too high on the LEM, a security disk had to burst if pressure was going high, but motor was unusable after. So it was changed on Apollo 19 and 20, but not tested in Space before. It was ok, but... in the paper. However, we got no problem with it. It was a long mission, 7 days scheduled on the Moon, every ray of light was used till ascent.

Apollo 19 had a loss of telemetry, a brutal end of mission without data. Now the truth is unknown but it seems that it was a natural phenomenon, a collision with a "quasi-satellite ", like Cruithne, or a meteor (the probability is higher I think). The goal was the same, the landing site was the same, the exploration program was different, they had a big job to do with the rover, exploring the roof of the ship by climbing on the "Monaco hill", (I'll have to put a lunar map online). NO American astronaut is listes, I discovered since may that many people find many William Rutledge in NASA. I can be found in the list of the Test pilots of Chance Vought, on the consultant list of the James Forrestal Center, I was involved in fluid mechanics. My boss was Bogdanoff (nothing in common with the Bogdanoff scientists).

Stephanie Ellis was born in Abidjan (Ivory Coast) in 1946, arrived in America at the age of 7 months. She was a LM specialist, she worked with Grumman Bethpage for new implementations on the navigation system of the LM (Note that LM15 was officially destructed by

---

6 The correct name is "Charles Pete Conrad", not Peter. "Pete" was just a nickname. Conrad was an astronaut of the second group of astronauts, chosen during the last century by NASA before they reached the Moon with a manned mission of landing.

Grumman). She contributed to debug the Luminary program, who was never bug free. Apollo 19 and 20 had serious problems with docking and rendez-vous. Her technical knowledge was as deep as Roger Chaffee. She was a wonderful and funny person. I have some pictures of her in the LEM and Ingress 16 mm footage. I'll not show the other members of the crew.

Russian collaborations; I don't know how, but Russian were informed of the presence of a ship on the far side. Luna 15 in July 1969 crashed just at the South of the nose of the ship. It was a probe similar to Ranger or Lunar Orbiter. They provided maps, precise charts of this area. The center of decision was located in the Ural, in the town of Sverdlovsk. The chief of the program was professor Valentin Alekseiev, who became later president of the academy of science in Ural. Leonov was chosen because of his popularity in the communist leading staff, and secondary only because he was on Apollo-Soyuz. In 1994, I met again Valentin Alekseiev in Ural, Yekaterinburg, and he had a model of the spaceship made of malachite with incrustations of gold on his desk.

I could tell you 100 stories about how Russians wanted to impress us. For example, when I came to the Academy of the Ural for the first time, my feet sticked on the ground, they had put varnish on the floor, not dried, for showing us new offices, they did all this "the Russian way", quickly, with quantity, not completely ready.

14) L.S. *Is there anybody in U.S.A., Russia or in Europe that can confirm your story? And are you not afraid that somebody can threaten your friends or relatives?*

W.R. In USA, honestly I don't know who is living now. Conrad died a strange way I think, his death was awful. Irwin is dead, von Braun also I think. James Fletcher. Leona Marietta Snyder is alive and communicates and support me in this job. In Russia, Valentin Alekseiev, and Alexei Leonov. Leonov is retired, I'm not sure of this but his health is a problem.

About security, no problem as far I live in Rwanda, I only have problem now in Europe, my family is dead. I went to Rwanda in 1990, and stayed during 3 wars, the April-July 1994 were the worst years of my life, but I have now true friends in the Tootsie community and Government. (I'm not known in Rwanda as William Rutledge and

American citizen, I have a whole new life).

I kept my moon flag, beta cloth name, and moon al7b equipment with original dust.

15) L.S. *What did you know about the unofficial Warwick Research Institute Report on the "Public Acclimation Program", released in 1992 to the MUFON?*

W.R. I have no knowledge of this report, 1992 was a very hard year for me, I was disconnected from all this, can you give me a link?

16) L.S. *Now we can discuss the ancient "alien spaceship" and "the City" on the farside of the Moon. Did you go inside the spaceship? How big was it and what did you find inside?*

W.R. We went inside the big spaceship, also into a triangular one. The major parts of the exploration was; it was a mother ship, very old, who crossed the universe at least milliard of years ago (1.5 estimated). There were many signs of biology inside, old remains of a vegetation in a "motor" section, special triangular rocks who emitted "tears" of a yellow liquid which has some special medical properties, and of course signs of extra solar creatures. We found remains of little bodies (10cm) living in a network of glass tubes all along the ship, but the major discovery was two bodies, one intact.

17) L.S. *Did you visit "the City" on the Moon? Where was it? Did you understand if was there a connection with the Space ship? Are "the City" and "the Ship" still there?*

W.R. The "City" was named on Earth and scheduled as station one, but it appeared to be a real space garbage, full of scrap, gold parts, only one construction seemed intact(we named it the Cathedral). We made shots of pieces of metal, of every part wearing calligraphy, exposed to the sun. The "City" seem to be as old as the ship, but it is a very tiny part. On the rover video, the telephotolens make the artifacts greater.

18) L.S. *What about the "Mona Lisa EBE"? [the correct Italian name is "Monna Lisa"] How does she look like and where was she at that time, when you found out her on the Moon. Where do you think she is now?*

29

W.R. Mona Lisa – I don't remember who named the girl, Leonov or me - was the intact EBE. Humanoid, female, 1.65 meter. Genitalized, haired, six fingers (we guess that mathematics are based on a dozen). Function; pilot, piloting device fixed to fingers and eyes, no clothes, we had to cut two cables connected to the nose. No nostril. Leonov unfixed the eyes device (you'll see that in the video). concretions of blood or bio liquid erupted and froze from the mouth, nose, eyes and some parts of the body. Some parts of the body were in unusual good condition, (hair) and the skin was protected by a thin transparent protection layer. As we told to mission control, condition seemed not dead not alive. We had no medical background or experience, but Leonov and I used a test, we fixed our bio equipment on the EBE, and telemetry received by surgeon (Mission Control meds) was positive. That's another story. Some parts could be unbelievable now, I prefer tell the whole story when other videos will be online. This experience has been filmed in the LM. We found a second body, destroyed, we brought the head on board. Color of the skin was blue gray, a pastel blue. Skin had some strange details above the eyes and the front, a strap around the head, wearing no inscription. The "cockpit" was full of calligraphy and formed of long semi hexagonal tubes. She is on Earth and she is not dead, but I prefer to post other videos before telling what happened after.

19) L.S. *Were you able to understand the origin of the spacecraft and how old was it?*

W.R. The age was estimated to 1.5 milliards of years, it was confirmed during exploration, we found ejections from the original crust, anorthosite, spirals in feldspathoids, coming from the impact which formed Izsak D; The density of meteor impacts on the ship validated the age, also little white impacts on the Monaco hill at the West of the ship...

20-21) L.S. *Can you give me the technical details for every material you disclosed on YouTube? I mean, can you distinguish among the tv transmissions from the Lunar rover and the camera footages, during the flyovers? I would need to know the details of shooting for every video you spread on the Web. What is the meaning of the strange numbers visible on the* *videos, which some*times slowly stream over the frames, in the flyover of the Moon?

W.R. I have answered so much time on this, especially to a ESA astronaut. The transfer was in made in Rwanda, [...] with codec and sound recuperation is not good, but it becomes better. The subtitles are not genuine, but put on the videos after transfer. I asked to remove the voices sometimes to protect one person from mission control.

We used three video cameras in Apollo, one on the rover, called GTCA, it is not the name of a company (a commenter made a mistake on this) but a Westinghouse color camera. All three color cameras has a color wheel who produced a time frame delay when transmitting to the earth. I think it could be possible for a company to restore a good TV picture. The CSM camera had a black and white monitor, and produced stable pictures, sharp because focusig was visible on the monitor. The LM camera had a glass visor. The CSM camera was used one time on the AGC Visor, using the coordinates I've transmitted during the flyover video. The Flyover video was made in zero gravity. I was located on the left window, attitude horizontal, legs around the hammock, lens on the polycarbonate glass. The cameras had a Vidicon tube sensible with light, a large quantity of light, or changing the diaphragms put dropouts during transmission. The markings, numbers are used to perform a good landing. During program 64, when [...] in almost in vertical attitude, we had to put the "60" number on the landing site and hold it on the target minutes before landing. These marks are on the both [...] windows, you can verify it on a NASA site. Please verify on a genuine NASA site, (I got a flame by somebody who verified on the Apollo 13 movie) the markings had a special angle inclination. If you check it, you'll have an idea of my precise position during this sequence.

22) **L.S.** *How did you get years ago the copies of the footages of the mission?*

W.R. About the footages [...] one day, someone I know told me he was charged to maintain security around a container. A building had to be destroyed, and archives had to be burn by a plasma torch. The nuclear power plant didn't deliver energy at the right price, so the container was plenty of interest things during some days. As human is naturally curious, people charged of security went inside... My friend took video films, a couple of 16 mm plates, boxes of B/W paper, two enlargers... He contacted me for selling the unsued paper, and that's how I discovered the other things. I've already seen some picture before, 11*16 pictures were violet/blue, old RC photographies, I watched the tapes , it was not a business affair, I put them in security, the only important thing for me were the BW sheets of paper. It was 15 years ago.

23) L.S. *Have you ever met Clark McClelland, former NASA engineer who lost his job years ago because of what he discovered at the KSC (I suppose alien bodies or alien objects from the Space)?*

W.R. But you can give me the links. Documents can be at KSC, but no bodies or alien craft I think.

24) L.S. *You mentioned in a former letter C. M. and M. Who are they?*

W.R. C. M. is the website officer on Oceans NASA site [http://oceancolor.gsfc.nasa.gov]; M. also. A. M. is 508 Coordinator. I only have mail exchange with Johnson Space Center for the moment. There is a moment of panic I think since May 18. Check 508 coordinator NASA on a search engine. Statement 508 is the way of pushing NASA to declassify material. I expected a reaction.

Luca >>> it is a part of my strategy, NASA has the right to block me if I download unauthorized information. If they explain why they block me, they recognize that the videos can be obtained from them. If I sue them for violation of Statement 508, they will be forced to prove I downloaded unauthorized material , and it's not the case, I never go on a NASA site.

Since May 18, I have not a precise answer, I have to wait for a decision from the headquarters.

Even as Italian citizen, you have the right to ask for material from a federal agency like NASA, see 508 Statement:

http://www.section508.nasa.gov/

25-26) L.S. *Aren't you afraid of the U.S. Government's reaction and why did you talk about the date of September 2007, when NASA and USAF* *(according to you) "will be forced to tell the whole story before September 2007" What does it mean and Who is your "deep throat"? In another recent your communication to me, you talked about the "2012" year. You said:*

<<In 2012, the weakers will die, and governments preserve the only bit of their heritage [...] everybody has to be prepared for 2012>>.

Is there any connection with the "Planet X" return (the ancient Nibiru, adored by the Sumerians in Mesopotamia) ? What did you know about it?

25   W.R.   I'm the deep throat. What can NASA USAF do now? Blocking or suing me would be an acknowledgement. They can speak of hoax or fiction. I'm just afraid they could open a site or another account with my name or putting almost perfect false videos with voluntary errors to disinform. Fortunately, bureaucracy and time works for me. It's a race.

That's why the idea of putting the Leonov files is a good idea, no controversy anymore, there are no Leonov footage, no videos of this period of Leonov in a LM or on a USA USAF base. It is unthinkable related to the official version.

26   W.R.   I am a passionate of the Sumerian period, of the Genesis as related by Sumerian. They clearly explain how gods created man. But I have no indications on Sumerian cosmogony, send me some links.

There is a question you didn't ask for and I'm always surprised that nobody does. This could be your question 27 - why is it necessary to hide UFOs, why disinformation, why putting all this under the carpet? It's question of economics. All currencies on Earth are based on the value of gold. Not many citizens know that but gold is an extraterrestrial metal coming from the death of a star. When a star is dying, its mass is growing, atoms are compressed and when the star explodes, it spreads large amounts of gold in young solar systems. That's why gold is not a mineral to treat but a perfect, carbon free metal. This mean that it is the most common substance in the universe, no more value than a piece of plastic.

That's enough to put down all world currencies. Imagine also that an EBE says: "coffee has a good taste, rare in this galaxy", the only perspective of trading coffee through universe would displace the economic power to countries of the South in one day. You see, not a problem of panic, but simply a problem of economy.

- The end of the interview -

May 25, 2007 www.angelismarriti.it Updating of images/captions October 2008.

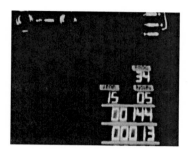 

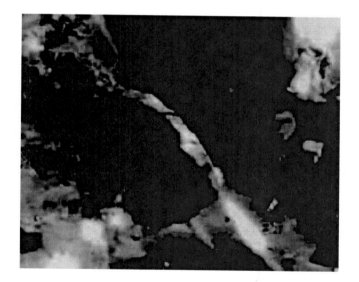

Snapshots (black and white, original colours deleted) from the footage

<<ALIEN SPACESHIP ON THE MOON flyover bef. landing APOLLO 20>> posted on May 4, 2007, on YouTube, by "retiredafb"; see Appendix II;

the first frames seem coming from an Apollo 11 footage; there is a video contamination, confirmed by the Apollo 20 Commander himself; on the left image, above, you can see the DSKY of an Apollo spacecraft; I discuss a possible reason for the contamination in the chapter XIII;

reproduction by kind permission of "retiredafb" (William Rutledge)

CHAPTER II

New Evidence Provided by William Rutledge, CDR of the Apollo 20 Crew

A few weeks ago I interviewed a man by the name of William Rutledge, who has been claiming his identity: he would have been an astronaut during the '70s, employed by the USAF in collaboration with NASA during a secret Space mission. My interview was carried out by my YouTube Account/General Messages. William Rutledge registered himself on YouTube as a man of 76 years old (YouTube user: "retiredafb"), who now lives in Rwanda. He told me he is an American citizen, now civilian, born in Belgium in 1930 and employed by USAF as test pilot on various aircrafts.

According to his report supported by some outstanding videos uploaded on YouTube since April 2007, after the Apollo 17 (December 1972) and the "Apollo18-Soyuz" mission taken place in July 1975, there were other two missions on the Moon: the Apollo 19 (failed because of <<*a loss of telemetry, a brutal end of mission without data*>>, see the interview with W.Rutledge) and the Apollo 20 (August 1976), which were both classifed Space missions launched from the Vandenberg Air Force Base (California).

Officially many Apollo missions were canceled by NASA during the Project Apollo, included the Apollo 20 (canceled in 1970).

The goal of these two presumed secret joint space mission, result of an American-Soviet collaboration, was to reach the backside of the Moon (the Delporte-Izsak region, close to the well-known Tsiolkovsky crater) and to explore a huge object found out during the Apollo 15 mission. What the Apollo 20 crew found, it was a huge and ancient alien spaceship, <<*approximately 4 kilometers long*>> (W. Rutledge).

And as a matter of fact, some official NASA pictures archived by the LPI (The Lunar and Planetary Institute in Houston), which is "a research institute that provides support services to NASA and the planetary science community" (www.lpi.usra.edu/lpi/about.shtml), show a strange and big object on the far side of the Moon. LPI is "is managed by the Universities Space Research Association (USRA)".

Here you are some of the details of those NASA pictures which show that cigar-shaped object:

 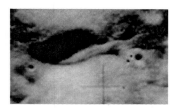

Details of Apollo 15 photos (AS15-M-1333 and AS15-M-1037 from the Apollo Images Atlas)
Image credit: The Lunar and Planetary Institute (LPI) - NASA Photos

Regarding the video entitled *"ALIEN SPACESHIP ON THE MOON flyover bef. landing APOLLO 20"*, on YouTube since May 4, 2007, as introduction we have a sort of marking with the presumed mission patch, which contains an interesting Latin inscription: <<*Carpent tua poma nepotes*>>. I realized later reading an essay of Latin quotations and sayings, that the Latin inscription on the presumed patch of the classified mission is from Virgilio's Bucoliche (IX, 50).

On the presumed patch we have the names of the crew as well: <<*Rutledge Snyder Leonov*>>, which is a typical NASA habit.

A couple of the footages are polluted with Apollo 11 recordings

But on the video of the flyover of the Lunar Module LM-15 (I checked on some Space history abstracts: the name of the spacecraft is coherent with the historical succession, because the Lunar Module Number begins from Apollo 5, with the LM-1, and for example for the Apollo 11 mission the name of the Lunar Module is LM-5; for some reasons not always the progressive number of the LMs is in accordance with the Apollo mission number), we have just a second of another marking about a video of the former Apollo 11 Mission.

The presence of an intrusive frame in the footage it would seem to be a contradiction, but perhaps it is just a result of a probable former recording on the film. According to William Rutledge (see my interview already mentioned), the first time he had to do with the footages was 15 years ago, because somebody he knew, charged to maintain security around a container, contacted him and told him what he found out inside (some <<*archives had to be burn by a plasma torch*>>).

I found another contradiction, which seems a sort of video pollution: the written comment by Rutledge about the video posted on April 9 and entitled "APOLLO 20 Legacy liftoff of Apollo 20 saturne 5", says: <<*Lift off of Apollo 20 saturn 5 from Vandenberg AFB august 16 1976. Note the marks on the rocket, different than the previous apollo launches.*>>

But the codec audio on YouTube is from the Apollo 11 mission. I'm sure about it, because I have carefully compared the video on YouTube with an official NASA video of the Apollo 11 lift-off. Rutledge, contacted by me about it, has confirmed the probable mixing. And it could be possible, if you consider that some of his friends in Rwanda are helping him in the transfer from the analogical films to the digital, and William Rutledge told me now he's not in Africa. So, if his friends have not a very good knowledge of the subject and of the Space history, they could make mistakes in assembling the codecs video with the codecs audio.

For the rest the Rutledge's report is enough coherent and plausible, and it shows a detailed knowledge of Aerospace history, of Geology, Chemistry and of Space exploration history, using specific terms. For example, he mentioned in the interview a not well-know term: the "feldspathoid", a "mineral consisting of an aluminous silicate that has too little silica to form feldspar" (*Webster's Third New International Dictionary*, Könemann, 1993,pag. 835).

Historical Evidence seem to corroborate the amazing story of the Apollo 20

1) **The Rockwell Corp. Logo on the overalls**

On June 18 2007 William Rutledge (with the help of his friends in Rwanda) uploaded on YouTube new evidence which seem to corroborate his amazing story: the *APOLLO 20 TEST Launch pad*, the *APOLLO 20 Test EVA 1* and the *APOLLO 20 TEST Snyder Ingress*.

For the last video here mentioned, W. Rutledge wrote the following text as comment: <<*Test Cinepak radius compressor. Rutledge and L. Marietta Snyder ingress*>>.

In the video you can see some technicians by a presumed launching pad for astronauts. In the footage (a capsule Ingress test?) they're helping two astronauts (who would be William Rutledge and Leona Marietta Snyder, former Bell Laboratories), who wear their space suits, to enter into a presumed spacecraft by a launching pad. The footage seems to be the editing of three different moments, in front of the entrance.

www.youtube.com/watch?v=wlMZU9XHSrU

The important point is that on the back of the technician's overalls, you can see what it seems the Rockwell corporation logo. Moreover, one of them has on the back the NASA logo. If you give a look to the Boeing's official website, you can find the following statement:

<< [...] *North American Rockwell designed and built the Saturn V second stage and the command and service modules.*>>

source: www.boeing.com/history/bna/apollo.htm

Moreover, besides to be the manufacturer of spacecrafts, that company (the Rockwell) planned and developed several military aircrafts. You can find more information on Wikipedia: <<*[...] North American was responsible for the famous WWII P-51 Mustang fighter and Korean War-era F-86 Sabre, as well as the Apollo spacecraft.*>>

source: en.wikipedia.org/wiki/Rockwell_International

Since the 1973 the name of the corporation changed: the North American Rockwell Corporation became the Rockwell International Corporation. W. Rockwell died in 1978, and since that time the corporation began a series of spin-offs. What remains of the company is the Rockwell Collins (COL) and the Rockwell Automation (ROK). The Rockwell International no longer exists.

Frames (b/w, original colours deleted) from the *APOLLO 20 TEST Snyder Ingress*
Video added by "retiredafb" (William Rutledge) on YouTube on June 18, 2007;
you can see the Rockwell Corp. logo; the video was removed later by
"retiredafb" himself.
reproduction by kind permission of "retiredafb" (William Rutledge)

2)   In the last Rutledge's footage, the capsul inside looks like an Apollo Spacecraft

The last video uploaded on YouTube by William Rutledge (retiredafb) on June 24, 2007, is really amazing: <<*APOLLO 20 ALIEN SPACESHIP ON THE MOON CSM FLYOVER*>>.

In the comment he wrote: <<*CSM 16mm footage through the AGC lens... CSM 16mm footage through the AGC lens, made by Leona Snyder [...]. Camera is fixed on the eyepiece of the telescope, less dropouts or moves than the Tv feed from the LM. Frame transfer is not perfect,speed is faster than actual, 4 different speeds were used on the 16 mm camera.*>>

40

Apart from the evocative 16mm footage by Leona M. Snyder in which you can see the details of the presumed abandoned alien spaceship on the far side of the Moon, during the flyover of the Apollo 20 CSM, in my opinion the decisive frames from the historical point of view are the first. At the beginning of the footage, in fact, you can see the Spacecraft controls and instruments. If you compare them, for example, with the 35mm photos available from the Apollo 17 Image Library of the Apollo Lunar Surface Journal, you will recognize almost every part of the capsule inside.

 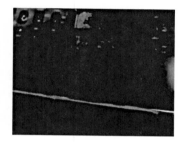

Frames in b/w (original colours deleted) from the
APOLLO 20 ALIEN SPACESHIP ON THE MOON CSM FLYOVER;
source: YouTube video, added by "retiredafb" on June 24, 2007;
reproduction by kind permission of "retiredafb" (William Rutledge)

Moreover, instead of the American flag, you have the union of the American with the Soviet flag, over the Apollo 20 patch. It does make sense using the same technology to go to the Moon, already tested with success, if you think that Apollo 17 mission took place at the end of 1972, as the presumed Apollo 20 in August 1976. And just the year before there was the well-known Apollo-Soyuz mission:

<<[...] Apollo 18 was the Apollo-Soyuz project, the honeymoon before a moon landing mission, it was presented as a simple "shaking hands " mission in 1975>>

(from the interview with W. Rutledge).

Waiting for the rest of the Rutledge's testimony, we should prepare ourself for the wait and new Copernican revolution: we are not alone in the Universe and, at last, historical and technical evidence are supporting it beyond any doubt.

What we need is an official declaration from Authorities. Perhaps, the American Code of Federal Regulations and the Public Law 91-76 created by U.S. Congress could help us to find the truth (see: history.nasa.gov/spacemedal2.pdf), together with a formal recommendation/petition to the NASA Administrator, to give a right recognition to the Apollo 19-20 crews.

It would be a good thing to disclose and spread the truth about the reality of the extraterrestrial intelligence in the Universe through an unknown historical fact in which the two great powers of the World of the past (the USA and the USSR) joined together for scientific and peaceful activities, in spite of all their differences and political hostilities.

As pointed out by William Rutledge in one of his comments on YouTube: << [...] the apollo 20 belongs to all mankind It is a part of all human's heritage>>.

Virgilio wrote: <<Carpent tua poma nepotes>>. The Apollo 20 patch quotes it. Maybe we are those grandchildren...

© L. Scantamburlo

June 26, 2007

www.angelismarriti.it

The titles of the article was corrected on August 20, 2007 and in October 2008.

L. S.

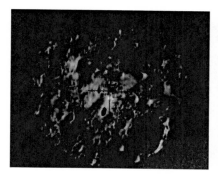

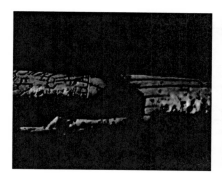

Frames (colours deleted) from the footage *APOLLO 20 ALIEN SPACESHIP ON THE MOON CSM FLYOVER*, taken aboard the CSM Constellation (Apollo 20): 16mm footage, through the AGC lens, by Leona M. Snyder;

footage provided by retiredafb on YouTube; video added on June 24, 2007;

reproduction by kind permission of "retiredafb" (William Rutledge)

[7]The comment added with the video on YouTube by "retiredafb", on June 24, 2007

<<*CSM 16mm footage through the AGC lens, made by Leona Snyder [...] lunar orbit revolutions. Camera is fixed on the eyepiece of the telescope, less than the Tv feed from the LM. Frame transfer is not perfect,speed is faster than actual, 4 different speeds were used on the 16 mm camera. The landing site is visible on the lower right part in the first lunar sequence. sorry for the first viewers and commenters, i had to upload again with a better codec*>>

---

7   Text reproduced from the original comment by "retiredafb", without any corrections. Video and comment were removed by "retiredafb" after a few weeks. Some letters – where I have put the dots - are missing here (not comprehensible).

CHAPTER III

Lunar Coordinates of the Alien Spaceship and Feature of the Fermi Walled Plane

The LM-15 flyover spread by W. Rutledge shows almost certainly the Fermi Walled Plane, close to the Izsak crater

A detail of the backside of the Moon
Image credit: The Lunar and Planetary Institute (LPI) - NASA

The LM-15 Flyover and the far side of the Moon

What can we understand about the astonishing footage of the presumed LM-15 flyover before descent on "Izsak D", spread on YouTube by William Rutledge on May 4, 2007? Is there any congruence between the visible details shown in the video footage and any lunar map of the far side of the Moon? For example, are recognizable the Fermi's details, or is recognizable any particular belonging to the lunar zone of the backside of the Moon, near the Izsak crater? In the comment posted by W. Rutledge ("retiredafb") on YouTube, we can read:

<<[...] LM passes over Tsiolkovski, Fermi, Delporte and Lukte before passing on the Izsak Y crater. [...] CDR communicates the South -East coordinates of the major parts of the spaceship, approximately 4 kilometers long.>>

A friend of mine from New York City pointed out months ago that, first of all, it would be a good result understanding if the LM-15 flyover really took place on the far side of the Moon, and moreover if there is any other video footage from NASA space missions which shows those surface details of the Moon.

What I have found is that there are some congruences if we compare the details shown in the frames of the LM-15 flyover footage, with an official lunar map available on the Lunar and Planetary Institute: the i_136_m.jpg picture which shows clearly the lunar details mentioned by William Rutledge: we have the Tsiolkovsky crater, the Lutke crater, and we can see the Delporte and the Izsak craters. Of course, it is visible also the large lunar crater by the name of Fermi, close to all the others and which belongs to the category named a walled plain.

Some features of the Fermi Walled Plane seem recognizable in the presumed LM-15 flyover

The Fermi walled plane has a diameter of about 183 km. During the presumed LM-15 flyover, the CDR (Commander) of the crew

<<[...] communicates the South -East coordinates of the major parts of the spaceship, approximately 4 kilometers long. Color distortions are caused by the rotating wheel inside the Westinghouse Color TV Camera.>>

What I asked to myself was if the there were something of recognizable. I watched very carefully the video footage entitled <<ALIEN SPACESHIP ON THE MOON flyover bef. landing APOLLO 20>>. The video footage lasts 5 minutes and 53 seconds. At a certain point I could recognize what, in my opinion, is the western border of the Fermi crater (a walled plane). It seems that the direction of the LM-15 is from Northeast to Southwest. As a matter of fact, when you watch the footage you should recognize the details of the western Fermi rocky border, high on the left of the screen, approximately after 2 minutes and 30 seconds from the beginning. The subititles of the footage which would be the radio communications between the Vandenberg AFB and the LM-15, say:

<< [...] Izsak is visible on the upper left side of the window [...]>>, a statement from the astronauts which is coherent with their position, with their route and with the features of the lunar surface visible during the flyover.

In a former point of the footage in the subtitles of the dialogues among the CDR and the Vandenberg AFB, we can read:

<<We passed over Tsiolkovsky, and we are over Fermi now [...]>>.

Again, it is a statement coherent with the fact that the two astronauts inside the LM-15 (W. Rutledge and A. Leonov) should be able to see on the lunar horizon the Izsak crater, on the upper left side of the window of their spacecraft. Now we can pay attention to the frames of the video footage. So, it is enough to take a couple of snapshots of the video footage, and rotating of 90° to the left. You will have, for example, the following frame: ILL.3.

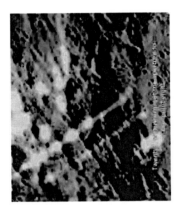

A (rotated) frame in black and white (coloured original frame, here deleted) from the footage of the LM-15 flyover before descent.

source: "retiredafb", YouTube

reproduction by kind permission of "retiredafb" (William Rutledge)

ILL. 3

First of all, with a free software (the Gimp software, version 2.2.10) we can delete the information of the colours; we can get the following image: ILL.4. And then we can change the brightness contrast of the picture.

Now, we can compare our little work with a detail of the i_136_m-LPI.jpg (changed in contrast), from the Lunar and Planetary Institute

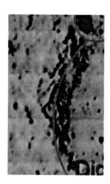

Detail of the i_136_m-LPI.jpg,

Courtesy NASA/LPI

Same detail, but changed in contrast

Even if the lunar zone is the same, because the shot equipment is different as well the date, the Sun position, the altitude of the spacecracft from which the shot was taken, it is obvious that we cannot have the same image results.

But it is very interesting that we can still recognize some paths in both pictures. So, almost certainly, we can say that at least the first minutes of the flyover are a really flyover of the backside of the Moon, over the Fermi walled plane and just close to the Izsak crater.

If you can consult the excellent photographic book *Full Moon* by Michael Light (© 1999 Jonathan Cape, Random House, London, © 1999 Michael Light), you can find a very important essay on the Moon by Andrew Chaikin (1950).

Dr. Andrew Chaikin was a former JPL scientist and he is author of the important book *A Man on the Moon* (1994). Chaikin in his essay talks about the astronaut's descriptions of the lunar surface, giving prominence to the fact that the lunar surface colours change very much under different conditions of light.[8]

Lunar coordinates of the Alien Spaceship are consistent with the position of the strange object visible in official NASA pictures

William Rutledge revealed that one target of the mission was landing by "Izsak D". I could not find any reference to that presumed particular Moon structure mentioned by him. I can suppose it is a Moon detail very close to the Izsak crater, and named like that by some space specialists involved in classified missions. But what about the the South -East coordinates of the major parts of the spaceship? Can we get any information from the coordinates provided by William Rutledge, Apollo 20 CDR?

The subtitles of the footage report the following data about the spaceship position: for the spaceship nose we have 17.3 deg S and 117.62 deg E, and for the spaceship cockpit we have 17.25 deg S and 117.62 deg E. So, it means that the presumed alien spacecraft is leant by the North-South axis, because what changes is the lunar latitude, while the lunar longitude of the two parts of the spaceship does not change. Moreover, the data tell us that the nose should be to the North of the cockpit.

---

8   This was a mistake of mine: the author who points out the different colours of the lunar surface, on the basis of astronauts' experience, is not Andrew Chaikin but Michael Light, who has written an essay entitled <<*La pelle della Luna*>> – the title in its Italian translation – for his photographic book *Full Moon*, Jonathan Cape, Random House, London, Michael Light, 1999. Italian edition: *Luna*, edited by Giovanni Caprara, Arnoldo Mondadori Editore, Milano, 1999. Translation by Guido Lagomarsino.

Now we can search for if there is any congruence among those data and the real position of the strange object visible on the official pictures taken by Apollo 15 and Apollo 17; strange and huge object that would be, according the story by W. Rutledge, an ancient and abandoned alien spaceship on the Moon. According to the index of the lunar charts of the The Atlas of the Universe (© 1970-1981, Mitchell Beazley Ltd London, Italian edition Cosmo, Istituto Geografico De Agostini, 1985) the Izsak crater has the following coordinates: latitude -23 Deg, longitude + 117 Deg, where the sign + means North, and the sign - means South.

The Alien Spacecraft's position regards as the Izsak crater and "Izsak D"

William Rutledge in his comments on YouTube gave us some information about "Izsak D" (where the alien spaceship was): it is to Southwest of Delporte Crater. If you combine that information with the following: <<DELPORTE, SOUTHWEST OF IZSAK, NORTH OF>> (from the AS15-P-9630 data, Apollo Image Atlas, NASA/LPI), we can understand that the spaceship is to North of Izsak, because in that NASA picture the presumed alien spacecraft is visible. Again, Rutledge's information are coherent with the position of the huge object visible in the official NASA pictures (taken from Apollo 15-17 missions). But for having the right position of the NASA picture as regards the lunar coordinates (latitute and longitude), we have to rotate of 90° to the left one of the NASA images of that lunar zone. If, for instance, we choose the AS15-M-1333 picture, we can get the following perspective: the illustration number 5 (ILL.5).

Detail of the AS15-M-1333, rotated to the left - The crater visible in the picture is almost for sure "Izsak D", which is close to the larger Izsak crater (not visible here)

Image credit: The Lunar and Planetary Institute (LPI) - NASA Photo

ILL. 5

I think that the operation is correct because I have compared the result to the already discussed i_136_m.jpg picture (from the Lunar and Planetary Institute) which shows clearly the lunar details mentioned by William Rutledge (Delporte, Fermi, Izsak, ect...) If you pay attention, you can recognize the form of the Izsak crater, and its position regards as the strange and huge object leant on the lunar surface, not visible in the i_136_m.jpg image but visible in the photos taken by Apollo 15-17 crews.

After all that I strongly believe the Apollo 20 mission revealed by the presumed William Rutledge, deserves the maxim attention of the scientific community, because its implications could broaden the mankind's horizons in every dimension, and also could reappraise the political and religious ideologies which have been still bringing on suffering and death on the Earth.

© Luca Scantamburlo

July 28, 2007

www.angelismarriti.it

Nose and cockpit of the presumed alien spaceship

For example, the Delporte crater is to the North of the Izsak crater: and in fact the Delporte's latitude is about -16° (16 deg S), when the Izsak's latitude is about -23° (23 deg S), which makes perfectly sense. So, it seems there is a contradiction in the subititles. Were the subtitles made by mistake, inverting the data because of too much hurry in typing?

W. Rutledge told us in the interview that some people (not him) made them in a hurry. So, it is possible a mistake. It is also true that everything depends on what portion of the object you consider as nose and what you consider as cockpit.

Other contradictions in the footage

A gentleman from USA, Mr. Charles Gilbert Wright, wrote me at the end of June because he found out that there is another contradiction that I had not noticed. He gave me his kind written permission to mention him: his discovery is analogous to that one I did about the audio coming from Apollo 11 lift-off, and put together to the presumed Apollo 20 lift-off (Vandenberg AFB, August 1976).

The short audio that we can hear watching the video named <<*Apollo 20 legacy part 1 The City*>>,

www.youtube.com/watch?v=qbncnnygZwk,

uploaded by retiredafb on April 07, 2007 and that would be *"Apollo 20 MET 140 22 29 the unscheduled trasmission rover TV"* by the Station One, it comes from a radio communication of the Apollo 15 mission; you can check on the following link:

www.hq.nasa.gov/alsj/a15/a15.lrvload.html

where at a certain point they say:

121:05:30 Allen[9]: <<*Presto chango; there's the TV.*>>

121:05:36 Scott: <<*Oh, beautiful, I'm glad to hear that.*>>

It is just the audio, not the video, which is probably what W. Rutledge

---

9   Joe Allen is mentioned as CAPCOM at Mission Control of Apollo 15, in the essay *More Than Earthlings*, by Colonel James B. Irwin, astronaut with Apollo 15 crew. At page 20 of the chapter 5 <<*Are You in Contact With God?*>>, Broadman Press, USA, 1983.

claims. But again, why there is an audio contamination? In my opinion it does not invalidate entirely his testimony. For example, if we give a look to the presumed <<APOLLO 20 ALIEN SPACESHIP ON THE MOON CSM FLYOVER>> video of the capsule interior, provided on YouTube by "retiredafb" on June 24, 2007, we can see that it was shot in a zero-gravity environment. We can argue that looking at the white straps sticking straight out, as one friend of mine pointed out. From the video that gravity is having no effect on the straps.

On the other hand, somebody could argue that the presumed Apollo capsule is in a museum. But in this case, who gave the permission to film such a fake? And why, if nobody is getting money from that?

The Apollo 20 case is still open. I hope the Rutledge's outstanding footages are a real effort of disclosure, in spite of there is something of controversial and contradictory.

If Apollo 19-20 missions took place indeed, other people involved could speak out for the advantage of the mankind.

© L. Scantamburlo

www.angelismarriti.it

The Izsak and "Izsak D" lunar craters

I have almost for sure localized the "Izsak D" crater, the target for the landing of the LM-15 of the presumed Apollo 20 mission (August 1976). At the beginning I was a little confused, because on a lunar map the Iszak crater looks like the other crater near the huge and mysterious cigar-shaped object leant on the lunar surface, on the backside of the Moon. The name of the Izsak crater comes from Imre Gyula Izsák (Zalaegerszeg, Hungary, 1929 - Paris, 1965), a Hungarian-American astronomer expert of celestial mechanics.

The Izsak crater has the following features:

Latitude: -23.3°

Longitude: 117.1°

Diameter: 30 KM

Source:

astrogeology.usgs.gov

www.lpi.usra.edu

But what about the "Izsak D"? But the "Izsak D" crater is not counted in the public lunar maps.

When we consider the official NASA picture AS15-P-9625 (taken on Apollo 15, 1971) where the curious object is visible, the Izsak crater is not shown, but on the other hand the crater in the middle of the picture is not explained or commented by NASA. That picture, which shows the portion of lunar surface indicated by the lunar map (9625), has the following details: Southwest of Delporte, North of Izsak; Latitude / Longitude: 19° S / 117.5° E.

If we compare that picture to the detail of the same zone of the lunar map available on the Lunar and Planetary Institute, we can see the Izsak crater is out of the borders of the picture.

So, it means that the "Izsak D" crater Mr. William Rutledge is reffering to, is probably the crater at the center of the AS15-P-9625 image.

Moreover, that consideration is enough coherent with the presumed dimensions of the spaceship (about 4 km long) and its dimensions and position regards as the Izsak crater, which is to the South.

© L. Scantamburlo

www.angelismarriti.it

Captions rewritten in October 2008.

CHAPTER IV

The Presumed Flight Course of the Phoenix Lunar Module Before the Descent

I am honoured to introduce you to the work by Haim Ram Bar-Ilan, the Israeli designer and artist who has already translated from English into Hebrew my interview with William Rutledge. You can find the interview on my website pages. See the link "interviews".

William Rutledge, whose nickname on YouTube is "retiredafb", has been claiming his identity since last Spring 2007: a former civilian test pilot on various aircrafts, born in Belgium in 1930 and employed in the last century with Avro, Chance Vought and USAF. In August 1976 W. Rutledge was, according his testimony granted to me in an interview, the Commander (CDR) of the Apollo 20 crew. That secret space mission was, always according to the Rutledge's testimony, a joint US and Soviet mission that followed by just over a year the joint Apollo-Soyuz Test Project (ASTP), taken place in July 1975.

Since April 2007 W. Rutledge added on YouTube several video footages which would come from the documentation material of that mission. One of them on YouTube has the following title: <<ALIEN SPACESHIP ON THE MOON flyover bef. landing APOLLO 20>>.

I have already discussed the video footage, that lasts 5 minutes and 53 seconds. At a certain point I could recognize what, in my opinion, is the western border of the Fermi crater (a walled plane). It seems that the direction of the LM-15 is from Northeast to Southwest. You can read my report entitled <<Lunar Coordinates of the Alien Spaceship and Feature of the Fermi Walled Plane>>.

Haim Ram Bar-Ilan (nicknamed "Rami") has recently identified, in the video spread by W. Rutledge, the Lutke crater. Here you are on this web page his first-rate reconstruction of the presumed flight course of the LM-15[10], the Phoenix Lunar Module. It would be the last revolution

---

10 Officially the LM-15 – the Lunar Module "Phoenix" according to William Rutledge, Apollo 20 CDR – has never flown and was scrapped. W. Rutledge knew this small detail of Space history, and he has pointed out in my interview with him (see the answer nr. 13). For a list of all LEMs spacecrafts produced in USA, see for example the website

before descent. And as a matter of fact, in the subtitles which go with the frames, we can read: <<[...] *and below os Lutke*>>. Of course "os" is a mistake: it would mean "us". The subtitles, W. Rutledge told us, were not made by him (see the interview).

And, we can add, not made by an English mother tongue either.

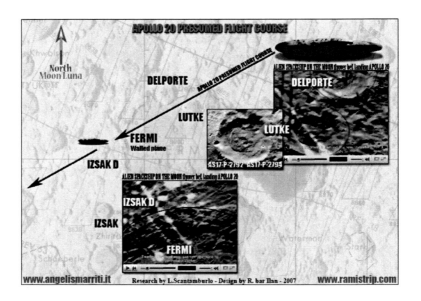

Reproduction by the permission of Haim Ram-Bar Ilan;
Research By L. Scantamburlo - Design by R. Bar-Ilan © 2007 - Thanks to YouTube

www.ramistrip.com

There are some controversial aspects in the Rutledge's testimony and material. But I am convinced that the story deserves our attention. Above all because of some difficulties I have met in doing my researches as journalist (for the moment I prefer not to spread them to the public).

Moreover, if the Apollo 19 (mysteriously failed with "a loss of telemetry") and the Apollo 20 did take place indeed, we should be very careful because it could begin a mass psychological warfare campaign

answers.com. The "Eagle" for Apollo 11 mission was the LM-5. For the Apollo 20 was the LM-15. All the LEMs were designed, made and tested by Grumman Corp. Now the company is part of the Northrop Grumman Aerospace System.

to destroy the testimony that William Rutledge gave us. If he is honest, we must remember he is risking his life, maybe. I like sharing my thoughts and considerations with some intelligent and honest people of the world: we have concluded together that because in the '70 years there was a huge and cigar-shaped object leant on the far side of the Moon, on this one piece of evidence, Natural Reason and Natural Law standing alone proves that we did go there. Thirtyone years ago, man had the capability to go there. We knew about the object from reconnaissance (by the Apollo 15 and Apollo 17 crews for sure, and perhaps even by the Soviet space probes).

Under Natural Law and Natural Reason, mankind had the duty, as a categorical imperative, to go there and investigate the mysterious object. You can be sure that it did happen. If it was not Apollo 20, it was some other secret space mission. And if somebody is skeptical about it, I invite him/her to read the Brookings' report, prepared in November 1960 by the Brookings Institution Washington, D.C.: <<*Proposed Studies on the Implications of Peaceful Activities for Human Affairs*>>, The report, prepared for NASA, was introduced to the Committe on Science and Astronautics by the House of Representatives of U.S.A. In the documents we can read:

<< *[...] Historical and empirical studies of the behavior of peoples and their leaders when confronted with dramatic and unfamiliar events or social pressures. Such studies might help to provide programs for meeting and adjusting to the implications of such a discovery. Questions one might wish to answer by such studies would include: How might such information, under what circumstances, be presented or withheld from the public for what ends? What might be the role of the discovering scientists and other decision makers regarding release of the fact of discovery?*>>

from pag. 216, ibidem

So it is clear that in the past somebody suggested several approaches and strategies about the steps to do in case of discovery of extraterrestrial intelligence in our Solar System. Included the possibility to withhold the truth of such a discovery "from the public."

© L. Scantamburlo

August 8, 2007

www.angelismarriti.it

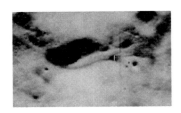 

On the left a detail of the AS15-M-1579 high resolution image, taken on Apollo 15 (camera altitude: 116 km); on the right, a detail of the AS15-M-1333 photo, rotated to the left. The crater visible in the picture is almost for sure the "Izsak D" crater, which is close to the larger Izsak crater (not visible here).

Images credit: The Lunar and Planetary Institute (LPI) – NASA Photos

Luca Scantamburlo – former Italian journalist - and

Haim Ram Bar-Ilan – nicknamed "Rami" - Israeli designer and artist.

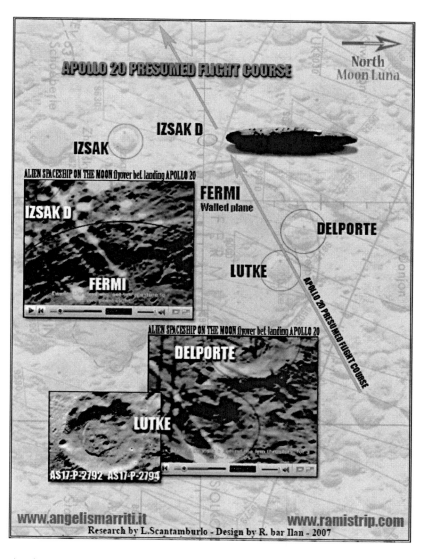

Another graphic work by Rami, where we can see the positiong of the cigar-shaped object. Reproduction by the permission of Haim Ram-Bar Ilan.
Research By L. Scantamburlo - Design by R. Bar-Ilan © 2007 - Thanks to YouTube

www.ramistrip.com

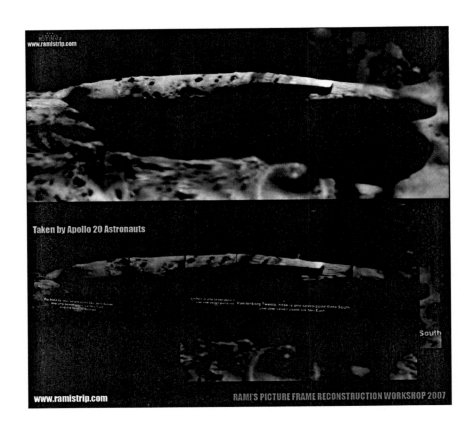

Another graphic work by Rami (original colours deleted), where we can see the huge cigar-shaped object close to the Izsak D crater, and here reconstructed through six frames from the flyover video

<<*ALIEN SPACESHIP ON THE MOON flyover bef. landing APOLLO 20*>>

Reproduction by the permission of Haim Ram-Bar Ilan.
Bar-Ilan © 2007

www.ramistrip.com

Lunar coordinates of the presumed alien spaceship

Source: the subtitles of the *"ALIEN SPACESHIP ON THE MOON flyover bef. landing APOLLO 20"*, video added by "retiredafb" on YouTube.

Far side of the Moon

Nose: 17.3 deg S, 117.62 deg E;

Cockpit: 17.25 deg S, 117.62 deg E;

Base: 17.20 deg S, 117.62 deg E;

Are the coordinates right? Were they given inverted? The longitude is coherent with the position of the huge object (approximately 4 km long, according to the subtitles of the YouTube video added by "retiredafb" (W. Rutledge). The problem is with the latitude: not with the latitude data, but with their reference to the major parts of the presumed "alien spaceship". Because we can see the base of the object is to the South of the nose, we should have, in my opinion, their reversal. It would be helpful to listen the original radio communication.

The marks for the CSM DSKY are from the transcription of the presumed dialogues between the Apollo 20 CDR and the Vandenberg Air Force Base. The Phoenix crew members, according to the "retiredafb"'s testimony, were A. Leonov and W. Rutledge. The base of the "alien spaceship" (the huge object shown in the image) is buried.

© L. Scantamburlo

August 8, 2007

www.angelismarriti.it

CHAPTER V

The Apollo 20 Case:
Debunking or a Trojan Horse
for the Truth?

"retiredafb", are you an impostor? Here his answer

Introduction to the controversial Apollo 20 case

Beginning in May 2007, I had many private contacts with a presumed William Rutledge (YouTube username, "retiredafb") who claims to have been a volunteer for MOL-Gemini project (he was not chosen, according to what he wrote me) and a former civilian test pilot on various aircrafts. Up to now my last contact with him, having always taken place by the YouTube General/Messages, was on July 20, 2007, at 01:39 pm: a message of just three lines.

Is he honest? Is he an agent of discredit? Is he a debunker? Who is behind him? Was he really a former test pilot who now is telling us the truth? Or just kernels of truth?

Rutledge could have been a former civilian test pilot on various aircrafts, born in Belgium in 1930 and employed in the last century with Avro, Chance Vought and USAF. According to his testimony granted to me in an interview, his last job before retiring was working on the KH-11 project.

Since April 2007 W. Rutledge posted on YouTube several video footages and images which could have come from the documentation material of a classified mission that took place in August 1976: Apollo 20.

He added 13[11] different videos; later he removed 4 of them. The main point of his presumed testimony was the probable space investigation of a mysterious cigar-shaped object, visible on official NASA photos

---

11 The exact number of videos uploaded by "retiredafb" on YouTube from April until June 2007, is 13, although two of them are very similar: *APOLLO 20 legacy part 1 The CITY* and *APOLLO 20 legacy part 1 The City*: different names, duration and codecs; See Appendix II at the end of the book.

taken by Apollo 15 and Apollo 17. The presence of the huge and mysterious object is a reality, based on fact, pointed out by Rutledge himself.

Under Natural Law and Natural Reason, mankind had the duty, as a categorical imperative, to go there and investigate the mysterious object. You can be sure that it did happen. If it was not Apollo 20, it was some other secret space mission. And if somebody is skeptical about it, I invite him/her to read the Brookings' report, prepared in November 1960 by the Brookings Institution Washington, D.C.: <<*Proposed Studies on the Implications of Peaceful Activities for Human Affairs*>>. The report, prepared for NASA, was introduced to the Committe on Science and Astronautics by the House of Representatives of U.S.A.

In the documents we can read:

<< *[…] Historical and empirical studies of the behavior of peoples and their leaders when confronted with dramatic and unfamiliar events or social pressures. Such studies might help to provide programs for meeting and adjusting to the implications of such a discovery. Questions one might wish to answer by such studies would include: How might such information, under what circumstances, be presented or withheld from the public for what ends? What might be the role of the discovering scientists and other decision makers regarding release of the fact of discovery?*>>

from pag. 216, ibidem

So it is likely that in the past somebody recommended and encouraged the adoption of several policies and procedures to follow should the discovery of extraterrestrial artifacts in our Solar System become a reality; chief among them: withholding or delaying disclosure of the discovery of such extraterrestrial "artifacts" from the public.

Contradictions and fakes. Did someone fabricate them on purpose to give us a riddle?

On July 01, 2007, at 01:33 PM, my YouTube account received a message from Rutledge. In his message the presumed William Rutledge answered my previous request for clarification. I was very upset because as time passed, many controversial aspects were coming out. I have already discussed them. Most of them are audio contaminations with radio dialogues from former Apollo missions (Apollo 11 and

Apollo 15). Finally somebody (a very clever YouTube user), discovered that the video of the presumed "City" (named "Station 1" in the interview) is a fake: if you examine images AS17-134-20437 and AS17-145-22163, found in the Apollo Image Atlas located at the Lunar and Planetary Institute website, you can see for yourself that the matrix of the lunar landscape (visible in the lower part of the screen) is a composition of images taken during the Apollo 17 mission.

On the left, AS17-145-22163 image taken with a 70mm Hasselblad; mission: Apollo 17, mission activity EVA 2; on the right, AS17-134-20437 image taken with a 70mm Hasselblad; same mission (Apollo 17), but from mission activity EVA 1;

Image credit: The Lunar and Planetary Institute (LPI) – NASA Photos

Frame from the footage entitled <<*APOLLO 20 legacy part 1 The CITY*>>, added on YouTube by "retiredafb" on April 1, 2007: it is a shot of a composition of images taken by Apollo 17 crew. So, the video is a fake, but made through official NASA pictures.

Image credit: "retiredafb", YouTube;

reproduction by kind permission of "retiredafb" (William Rutledge)

Even if the lunar features visible in those images could be signs of artificial structures, they do not refer to the Izsak's neighbourhood. They are images taken by the Apollo 17 crew, who landed on December 11, 1972, on Taurus-Littrow region (coordinates: 20°9'55" N and 30°45'57" E).

But there is the slight possibility that the fake was fabricated on purpose to provide us with a clue in investigating a lunar anomaly: is it possible that the main "rocks" in the image (i.e., rocks having 90-degree angles) are remains of some artifacts? Could the lunar hills in the background be pyramid-like structures, with steps going up the side, like in Mexico City, but partially obfuscated by a thick layer of dust? The site is obviously very old.

However I am aware that now the contradictions of the Apollo 20 case are too many to be simple mistakes made by inexperienced helpers who would live in Rwanda (the country that Rutledge has been claiming as his place of residence).

"retiredafb", are you an <<impostor>>? - Here his answer

In my quest for answers, I had previously posed the above question mentioned in the title of the paragraph even before to know the truth about the "City" footage spread by "retiredafb" (I received the initial signaling in August, through a gentleman in Portugal). In my question I used the nasty word "impostor", as a possibility for explaining this controversial case, which however gave us the opportunity to discuss the presence of an unknown object on the far side of the Moon. I had asked him to provide me more technical and heretofore unknown historical details that could prove his identity of being a former test pilot and Apollo pilot above all to face the suspicion which was growing in my mind: the idea that maybe he were an impostor.

In his answer "retiredafb" mentioned two NASA employees who, according to him, replied to an e-mail sent them. In this article I am not going to name them. But they are NASA employees indeed. I have checked their names; nevertheless, I decided to omit them (see the dots in brackets) due to the contradictory aspects of the case and the fact that I have not received enough evidence of the alleged e-mail exchange yet, and not to mention respect for the privacy rights of persons in question here. Moreover, the presumed William Rutledge has never used his e-mail address with me. He contacted me only through my YouTube Account /General Messages. So that you might thoroughly examine the issue and draw your own conclusions, I am incorporating the following excerpt from the original message (without any kind of correction of possible mistakes) "retiredafb" sent to my YouTube account:

> <<Only [...] and [...] wrote me. About details confirming the story, i could give you some things unknown on internet or in books, details that nasa could confirm, if they still have some people active and with a good knowledge of apollo program. - The american flag used during apollo 17 , was the backup flag of the apollo 11 crew. Aldrin and Amstrong used it on the ground, in the KSC building during EVA training. This same flag is now on the ground of the moon, stucked near the steno crater. This old apollo 11 flag is in Taurus Littrow site, Gene Cernan or Harrisson Schmitt can confirm that, or Nasa maybe, but it is a detail omitted in space history. -During Apollo 20, during the REFSMMAT procedure, we used stars for aligning the LM. Three of them were named REGOR NAVI and DNOCES. These names are not recognizable on any sky chart, they were the nicknames of the three astronauts dead during Apollo 1, but spelled backwards. REGOR was ROGER, "roger Chafee" NAVI was IGOR "Virgil IVAN Grissom", and DNOCES meaned SECOND for Edward Higgins White the second. I dont remember what was the number corresponding during REFSMMAT.>>

from the retiredafb's message to Luca Scantamburlo, July 01, 2007, at 01:33 PM - Scantamburlo's account /General Messages, YouTube

The REFSMMAT procedure and the Apollo 1 crew

I did not know what the REFSMMAT acronym meant. So I checked on some encyclopaedias and I have found they are initials indicating the procedure used by guidance, navigation, and control system flight controllers during the Apollo program. The term stands for: "Reference to Stable Member Matrix". More information is available on a NASA website: <<[...] a reference orientation which can be well defined and used by the crew in their platform alignments.>>

source: http://history.nasa.gov/ap15fj/02earth_orbit_tli.htm

On the link you find the "Star Reference ListNumber" and the Star name which Rutledge is reffering to in his message. Rutledge does not remember the numbers (of course if he is honest at least on this issue); they are the following: 03 for "Navi", 17 for "Regor" and 20 for "Dnoces".

The point is: again we have some very interesting technical details (not well-known among the general public) provided by William Rutledge, and again we have a statement by Rutledge which is not without contradictions: his historical recollection is true, but is reported by some websites; for example in the following:

http://www.space.com/spacewatch/star_names_030829.html

On another one we can read:

<<[...] the first Apollo crew used their own names spelled backwards Navi = Ivan Grissom, Dnoces = Edward White II, and Regor = Roger Chaffee. When they died in the fire, their unofficial names became used in many different ways. The October 1994 Sky and Telescope magazine apparently has an article on this subject.>>

source: <<Are there stars called Novi, Regor and Dnoces?>>

www.astronomycafe.net/qadir/ask/a11234.html

The Apollo 1 crew died in a tragic accident on January 27, 1967, during a launch pad test of the Apollo/Saturn spacecraft being prepared for the first piloted flight: the AS-204 mission. Subsequently the AS-204 mission was redesignated Apollo 1 to remember the lost space crew.

The three crew members were: Lt. Col. Edward Higgins White II (1930-1967), Lt. Col. Virgil Ivan "Gus" Grissom (1926-1967) and Lieutenant Commander Roger Chaffee (1935-1967).

About the American flag used during Apollo 17, I could not find anything to corroborate or to controvert the information given me by "retiredafb" (William Rutledge). So I think it is necessary to investigate the presumed historical details provided by William Rutledge. This is the main goal of SpaceHeroes.org. One of its team members found out an interesting public document.

The Saturn V listed by USAF in the Energy Space Assets

The document mentioned above is a .ppt presentation prepared by Dr. Ron Sega, Under Secretary of the U.S. Air Force. The date of the document is April 19, 2006, and the title is: <<*Air Force energy Strategy*>>. On page 16 you have the Energy and Space Assets prospect: the Saturn V rocket is mentioned, and there is also the comparison with dates: the year 1970 and the year 2006. The fact that the Apollo 20 would have been launched from Vandenberg AFB, according to Rutledge's testimony, is now supported by strong circumstantial evidence.

Moreover, there are official documents (from the '60 years) which prove that the USAF officials discussed and boosted the use of the Saturn V rocket. There is a specific point where the subject is: <<*Saturn V/Apollo Spacecraft Guidance Computer Developments Programs*>>. Why? It is obvious that the USAF needed the Saturn V capability in case USSR began to set up bases on the Moon. This was probably the main motivation for going to the Moon, and to counter Soviet threat of going there and exploiting it militarily.

Behind the William Rutledge's identity: the "strategy of confusion"?

Is it possible that behind the William Rutledge's identity there is an agent of some Secret service of an European country who is trying to push (or to drive), the US Government to reveal what it knows about the possible extraterrestrial presence in the Solar System? Or is he a person in control of some shadow Government scheme to subject the public to a psychological and sociological test in the context of the unofficial and rumoured "Public acclimation program"?

So, if Apollo 19 and Apollo 20 missions really took place and one of the crews members is now collaborating to spread the truth, it is obvious that spreading classified material on YouTube would be a military and diplomatic problem. So the better thing to do could be, in that case, spreading true information about the secret space missions but mingled with fakes and contaminations (always using official space documentation).

In my opinion, in spite of the contaminations and contradictions of the case, there are some important questions without a conclusive answer:

1) How did "retiredafb" know about the huge cigar-shaped object resting on the far side of the Moon, visible on official NASA pictures (taken on Apollo 15 and Apollo 17)?

2) How did he get secret video footage? Some of them are in the public domain and therefore are not secret (they are from former Apollo missions); but some of them, up to now, look like genuine footages never revealed to the public. I am talking about the *APOLLO 20 TEST Snyder Ingress* (added and later removed by "retiredafb") and the first part of the presumed LM-15 flyover (*ALIEN SPACESHIP ON THE MOON flyover bef. landing APOLLO 20*). Of course in the future new elements could come out and change my prospect;

3) How did he know about "Section 508", an official NASA section in charge of providing information?

4) How could a simple joker know so many technical aspects of space history and space flight? I believe that in such a case it would be necessary to have a strong support from someone.

So the presumed Apollo 20 disclosure could very well be only a step of the so-called "strategy of confusion": a strategy which could avoid panic and uncomfortable questions for the Authorities. In my opinion with this sort of Trojan horse (the Apollo 20 case), it would be possible to diffuse a secret truth crucial to the future existence of the mankind while, at the same time, satisfying public curiosity in the far side of the Moon and its mysteries without concern or worry about the eruption of diplomatic intrigue should the real truth be disclosed.

© L. Scantamburlo

August 22, 2007

www.angelismarriti.it

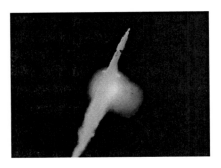

Frame (colours deleted) from the footage

APOLLO 20 Legacy liftoff of Apollo 20 saturne 5,

added on YouTube by "retiredafb" on April 9, 2007

Was it the rocket launched from the Vandenberg AFB, on August 16, 1976?

The audio associated with this video, is coming from some Apollo 11 footage; it means that for sure we have a contamination, for some reasons; fake or an authentic lift-off from the Vandenberg AFB, in the West coast? We can remark the clean sky, with little damp air;

Image credit: "retiredafb", YouTube;

reproduction by kind permission of "retiredafb" (William Rutledge)

"retiredafb": his YouTube profile, added on April 1st, 2007

<<*Videos of the boldest and most secret apollo mission. Apollo 20 went to the moon august 16 1976. Destination was Iszak D, southwest of Delporte Crater, farside of the moon. The mission was soviet-american. Crew was William Rutledge CDR, former of bell laboratories, leona snyder CSP bell laboratories, and alexei leonov, soviet cosmonaut former "apollo soyouz" (mission one year earlier). Station 1 on the moon was "the city"; Station two was "the ship". During the four EVA, LMP and CDR brought technical objects from the ship and a body, on of the two pilots of the alien spaceship. The body, the city and the ship were very old, age has been estimated 1.5 billion of years. Meteorit impacts, and dust/hills coverings testified that. Note that the ship has already been explored before the first human expedition reached the lunar singularity.*>> [12]

http://www.youtube.com/profile?user=retiredafb

Style: Commentary, Joined: April 01 2007, Age: 76, City: gisenyi, Country: Rwanda

---

12 Text reproduced from the an original comment by "retiredafb", without any corrections. The text of his user-card on YouTube was revised by "retiredafb" many times. The name of Soviet cosmonaut Alexei Leonov, for example, was written, removed (censored with X letters), and again re-written later (for example, on November 5 2007, the name was deleted; i.e. on December 7, 2007, the name was visible again on the comment posted on his YouTube profile). The reason for that will be clear for the reader when he will read my comment about it.

CHAPTER VI

Apollo 19 and 20:
New Clues and Revelations On the Case

Clues on the William Rutledge's identity

Could "retiredafb" - YouTube user who claims to be William Rutledge, now 77 years old - have been a former civilian test pilot on various aircrafts? He told us this and other things: that he was born in Belgium in 1930 (in Grembergen, he specified in his user-card on-line on YouTube) and that he was employed in the last century with Avro, Chance Vought and the USAF, before taking part in Apollo 20, a classified mission to the Moon alleged by him to have taken place in August 1976 from Vandenberg AFB aboard a Saturn V moon rocket.

It is entirely possible that Apollo 20 could have been a secret joint US and Soviet space mission that occurred one year after the famous Apollo-Soyuz Test Project, which launched in July 1975.

According to his testimony granted to me in an interview, Rutledge's last job before retiring was working on the KH-11 project (USAF). He explained me also that the ASTP (Apollo-Soyuz Test Project) was the preparatory mission to Apollo 19; and later Apollo 20, after the presumed failure of Apollo 19 and the loss of its crew. He told me that the ASTP was, for the Americans, the Apollo 18. Is it possible and correct under the historical point of view? Let us begin by examining the historical record.

Apollo 18? Yes, it did exist and it did take place

As the matter of fact, an official NASA Web page with an indication that ASTP was a mission involving Soyuz 19 and Apollo 18 capsules, can be found at the following link:

http://www.hq.nasa.gov/office/pao/History/apollo/welcome.html

The caption "Apollo 18" identifies who the United States crew members of the ASTP were: Thomas P. Stafford, Vance D. Brand, Donald K.

"Deke" Slayton. Although we have no evidence in the historical record that Apollo 18 was followed by Apollo 19 (due to Apollo 19 being most a secret USAF mission), William Rutledge gave a precise definition for the ASTP. It was correct, in spite of the fact this information is not well-known by the general public.

The KH-10 and KH-11 projects

According to William Rutledge, his last job before retiring was working on the KH-11 project (see my interview to him, answer n. 7). Moreover, he told us that he was a volunteer for the MOL-Gemini program (see his answer n.4), but he told me in a private YouTube communication he was not chosen.

From the historical record, MOL means "Manned Orbiting Laboratory", and was a program created by the USAF (not NASA) to put Air Force pilots in Space for periods up to 40 days. Canceled in 1969, the MOL program was replaced by the KH-11 program. Due to the need to surveil the entire surface of Earth, MOL-Gemini was designed so it could be launched from Vandenberg AFB (for insertion into polar orbit). I have found that MOL was also known as KH-10 (code name: "Dorian"). This is what surprised me because Rutledge did not mention MOL-Gemini as KH-10, but he mentioned KH-11. Thus, we can conclude that what William Rutledge's account of his involvement as potential pilot for the MOL-Gemini (KH-10) and his participation to KH-11 program as an employee before retiring, comports with the historical record.

The KH-11 (code name: "Crystal") is a series of military satellites launched from Vandenberg AFB from December 1976 until the end of the '80s, and were used as reconnaissance satellites placed in polar orbit for global surveillance purposes.

If you are interested in obtaining more information on the issue, visit the F.A.S. website (*fas.org*). Formed in 1945 by some atomic scientists and engineers from the Manhattan Project, F.A.S. is an acronym for Federation of American Scientists and was created by them because they knew just how important it is to provide information to the public to help encourage and facilitate discussion on critical national decisions.

His birthplace: Grembergen, Belgium

What can be said about his presumed birthplace in Belgium? William Rutledgte updated his YouTube card at the beginning of June 2007- if I remember well - when he added as his birthplace the name "Grembergen", but between brackets. I have checked on some encyclopaedias and on the Web: Grembergen is a small Belgian town close to Dendermonde, in Oost-Vlaanderen region. They speak French and Flemish languages, the two official Belgian languages. Oost-Vlaanderen is the Eastern Flanders, where Grembergen is located.

About the retiredafb's presumed surname (Rutledge), I received some help from South America: an engineer (G.C. - he asked me not to mention him, with exceptions oh his initials) wrote me an e-mail about it. He recommended that I search for the surname, "Rutledge", at familienaam.be, a website where you can find a geographical diffusion of a Belgian family name. So I have found two zones in which the family name "Rutledge" is present, or perhaps native. In one of them there is Antwerp city (in Italian we say "Anversa"). But Antwerp is a city near Grembergen: only 27.3 km by air and 33.6 km by road. You can check the distances using, for example, Microsoft AutoRoute.

This is an interesting clue. If "retiredafb" is a faker and an impostor, he has chosen very well his presumed surname and place of birth, coherent with the geographical diffusion of the family name, "Rutledge". Otherwise, I guess we have a piece of evidence which indicates he indeed does exist and that he is most likely a Belgian man by the name of William Rutledge, who became later an American citizen.

The main question is: was William Rutledge really a civilian former test pilot and astronaut who worked as contractor for USAF in the '70s? (today, for instance, the Blackwater security firm and its activities for the DoD are well-known, as Kevin Smith pointed out during his radio talk show with me as guest, at the beginning of October 2007).

About the Apollo 19 and the Luminary Program: detailed knowledge of the Apollo Program

In recollecting the dramatic loss of the Apollo 19 spacecraft and its crew, it was amazing thing to me how William Rutledge was more precise about it before what he told me in the interview (see answer nr.13); on May 23 he told me in our contacts (see Fig.3) that:

> <<Apollo 19 had a loss of telemetry wheile being at the end of the TLI, it was not clearly explained at this time, but it is beleived, it was a natural phenomemon, a collision of the aircraft and one of Cruithne brother, who was not identified in 1976. >>

May 23, 2007, 06:12 PM, from my YouTube Account

I did not know what TLI meant, and I have found later that it is the acronym used to indicate the propulsion maneuver which sets a spacecraft on a trajectory which will intersect the Moon. TLI stands for "Trans Lunar Injection".

> <<[...] In 2 hours and 38 minutes, the J-2 engine on the aft end of the S-IVB stage is due to be restarted in a maneuver that will send Frank Borman, Bill Anders and Jim Lovell further away from the Earth than any human has ever ventured. This is the TLI or Translunar Injection maneuver.>>

http://history.nasa.gov/ap08fj/02earth_orbit_tli.htm.

Another thing that surprised me is what I have found about the data Rutledge gave us in the interview (see answer nr. 10). Here you have his original words I received on May 25, 2007, again without any correction:

> <<[...] CSM is command module service, DSKY was the computer "display keyboard", we used many acronyms .AGC is apollo guidance computer, same that dsky, but located in the apollo spacecraft and coupled with a telecope (aot on the lm).In some videos, the first image you see is the dsky pannel with lines prog indicates the program running verb and noun verb indicates what the dsky has to do and show. Before filming i had to enter verb 15 (display MET, mission elapsed time, or hours minutes seconds since liftoff, then noun 65 for displaying on therre rows, hours on the first line minutes ont the second, and seconds/tens of seconds on the third line). Then i had to film the creen to date the tape. >>

May 25, 2007, 07:06 PM, from a retiredafb's message to my YouTube Account.

So I checked on the Apollo 15 Delco LM Manual - LM DSKY, that you can consult on-line because there is the PDF version of the full Delco LM Manual (181 Mb) created by Frank O'Brien. Moreover, there are some pages which were extracted from the PDF version

http://www.hq.nasa.gov/alsj/a15/a15LMDSKY.html

It is enough to choose the right files (verbs and nouns)

In this case I downloaded the A15DelcoLM-11 and the A15DelcoLM-06 JPEG images. Yes, Rutledge said something right. Verb 15, in the list of verbs used in Program Luminary, means "Monitor Octal Components 1, 2, 3, in R1, R2, R3", while the noun 65 means "Sampled LGC time (fetched in interreput)

00XXX. h

000XX. min

0XX.XX sec

Again, it seems William Rutledge knew something consistent with space flight concepts and particularly with Program Luminary (see also the interview to him, answer nr. 13).

About Roswell, reverse engineering and triangle spacecrafts on the Moon

I want to point out that the presumed former test pilot (William Rutledge), before he granted me the interview, in our private contacts told me something I did not made public yet. You can imagine how I felt months ago, and why I did not reveal the information. I was a little skeptical and shocked at the same time. As journalist I am aware that I must protect my source of information, but also spreading information and evidence which can help the public to understand how much truth there is in the case. So, I will not spread any information which can compromise his life or causing troubles to someone else.

It does not matter if he is really a former test pilot or just an impostor. Ours was a private communication, with some portions of it for sure destined to the public. Though I have the feeling he told me many things because he wanted to make them public, and I know that it is in the public interest collecting evidence and details for our understanding, I have to be very careful in spreading his information.

What did William Rutledge tell me? Rutledge told me something about the UFO cover up, about J.F. Kennedy's assassination (he put a wrong date on his message: 1961 instead of 1963, but if W. Rutledge is not an impostor, it could be just a so-called lapsus calami committed by an old man, a common mistake that everybody does at least once in the life) and about reverse engineering carried out in USA, after retrievals of 6 alien spacecrafts crashed between Alamogordo and Roswell, in 1947. Moreover he also mentioned Corso to me, and something about the propulsion system of the alien spacecrafts. This occurred on May 23, 2007, before the interview. Here you are some of his original words, without corrections: <<[...] six craft fel on earth between alamogordo and roswell, 5 in alamogordo>>

I am going to spread these information (true or false I do not know yet) to the public in the future, but before that, I want to write an affidavit for *SpaceHeroes.org*, in which almost every our communication taken place on YouTube will be a single exhibit.

About triangular spacecrafts on the far side of the Moon, and about the reasons for he decided to speak out, Rutledge said to me :

<<[...] about the spacecraft, one triangle was accessible) in a triangle craft, we found two bodies, one in bad condition, a meteor cut the body at the neck level, we tok the littl skull on board. The other body was strange, NDNA, not dead not alive, but crusted with impacts, stalagmites of blood coming out of hemmoragias zones. One body was on apollo 20, fixed on a hammock, and we passed hours watching the hands, the strange hair, not the kind you see a scifi movie. The hair was in good condition, we can say alive, alexei tested it.The ship was not explored on the 4 kilometers, but no place detected for weapons.>>

May 23, 2007, 07:42 AM, from a retiredafb's message to my YouTube Account.

<<[...] -no military craft, exploring one, Crew of 300, two female pilot on trangles. [...] I choosed to to it know because all apollo program had to be definitely locked with th outgoing of 'the marvel of it all' presented april 20, presenting the 12 astronauts alive who stayed on the moon.

I t was a trahison for me , for alexei, and for the 3 dead astronauts of amollo 19. My girlfriend Stephanie ELlis, first american woman in sace, fisrt afro maerican woman was killed during this mission, i have no place to *pray for her, her remains are still in orbit around earth.>>*

May 23, 2007, 07:48 AM, from a retiredafb's message to my YouTube account

New considerations on the dimensions of the cigar-shaped object on the far side of the Moon

As dr. Carl Sagan used to say (see his television program "Cosmos"), science is a self-correcting process. Of course journalism is not science, but I guess the principles are valid and apply the same way. Let us begin from a mistake I made while I was discussing on the controversial Apollo 19/20 case.

At the end of October 2007 I was spokesman at a conference organized in Lucca, a city close to Florence (Italy). The evening topic was the dark side of the Moon and the presumed Apollo 20 mission, officially never occurred. Another spokesman of that evening was completely not in agreement with me. In spite of the deep throat by the name of William Rutledge ("retiredafb" on YouTube) has pointed out a huge cigar-shaped object on the far side of the Moon, he declared the Apollo 20 mission completely a fake. According to him, even that object is a result of a natural phenomenon that took place on the lunar surface in the distant past.

The strange thing is that he made some calculations to estimate the object dimensions, and he obtained some results which indicate the object is longer than what we thought (see the Salvatore Valentin Carta's assessment: lenght of 3.370 km and width of 0.510 km). Because the Italian spokesman referenced Izsak crater as the crater immediately close to the cigar-shaped object, using it as ruler, I believed his result was wrong. As the matter of fact that crater is not the Izsak crater; it is what W. Rutledge has indicated as "Izsak D" - it looks like a double impact crater, which appears as a figure eight-shaped crater. But as a coincidence its dimensions are almost like Izsak crater dimensions, which are known by the scientific community. So that evening in Lucca city I was correct about the Izsak crater position, but I was incorrect about the lenght of the so-called "spaceship" resting on the backside of the Moon.

Whatever that strange object is (a strange natural formation or an alien spacecraft), its length is more than 4 km. We can safely say between 3 and 5 km. William Rutledge told us that is approximately 4 km long.

I can say this because after that conference in Lucca, I worked on the pictures by myself to measure the pixels of the objects. First of all, I downloaded a free software: ZoomMagic (Copyright PeakStars). With ZoomMagic you can measure objects dimensions in pixels and in centimeters. We know that the Izsak crater is in the South-East lunar quadrant, on the backside of the Moon.

Of course, for this reason, is not observable from the Earth. Its dimension are: 30x30Km / 18x18Mi; you can check on the Virtual Moon Atlas, a free software under the GNU General Public License (database © Ch. Legrand) very well done and useful. Otherwise, you can check by the astrogeology.usgs.gov database.

So we can use Izsak as ruler. I have chosen a JPEG image listed as AS15-M-1720, from the Apollo Image Atlas (LPI). it is a Hi Resolution Image (2.9 MB): (Width) 2400 x (Height) 2397 pixels.

We can think of the longitudinal axis of the cigar-shaped object as the hypotenuse of a right-angled triangle. I have measured the two catheti: 16 pixels and 67 pixels. To find the hypotenuse we can use the well-known Pythagoras theorem: I have got the value of 68.88 px. With a simple ratio we can calculate the dimension in km of the huge object of the far side of the Moon:

430 (px): 30 (km) = 68.88 (px): X (km)

What I got is: x= 4.80 km. X in this case would be the object lenght, considering the approximation that the cigar-shaped object is parallel to the lunar soil, and that there is no perspective effect in the picture. So we have a lenght of almost 5 km.

My feeling is that huge object is not a natural formation and if there is the tiny possibility it is artificial, it was and it is mandatory for mankind to investigate that lunar anomaly with a robotic or a manned mission on the far side of the Moon.

© L. Scantamburlo

November 8, 2007.

www.angelismarriti.it

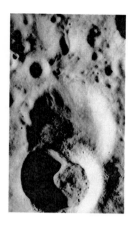

A detail of the NASA picture listed as AS15-M-1720, but rotated of 90°; the eight-shaped crater, is probably the presumed "Izsak D" crater mentioned by "retiredafb"

Image credit: The Lunar and Planetary Institute (LPI) - NASA Photo

Izsak crater, diameter: 30 KM

it is a detail of the image AS15-M-1720 taken from an altitude of 114 km (Apollo 15 mission); Camera Tilt: VERT; Revolution: 44; Sun Elevation: 20°;

Lens Focal Length: 3 inch

Image credit: The Lunar and Planetary Institute (LPI) - NASA Photo

CHAPTER VII

An Increase of
Celestial Phenomena

William Rutledge warned me in year 2007,

before the evident increase of celestial phenomena

In December 2007 the American website *alienseekernews.com*[13] published online my article entitled <<*What Is Going on in Space? William Rutledge Warned me About an Increase of Celestial Phenomena*>>. You should be able to find the text on my website, at the link "reports-articles".

In that article I pointed out that the mysterious and alleged Apollo 20 Commander - William Rutledge, a.k.a. "retiredafb" on YouTube – in our previous contacts had made some revelations during the spring and the summer 2007, but that I had not discussed them yet, until December 2007.

Those already disclosed before the last month of the year 2007, were in my interview with him: an increase of UFO sightings (<<*UFOs will appear more often starting from September 2007*>>, see the answer nr. 6) - a prevision which seems confirmed through last data on UFO phenomenon occurred in the years 2008 and 2009 - and a disclosure by NASA and USAF on the Apollo 20 case within a few months, prevision not come true (NASA and USAF would have been <<*forced to tell the whole story before September 2007*>>, see the questions nr. 25-26 of my interview with him.

In that article written by me in December 2007, I had decided to publish some snapshots of our private messages (censored by me in some points) to provide an evidence for the general public, otherwise it would have been very hard to believe me. So, in spite of at that time I had not enough evidence to prove he was a former test pilot involved in some secret space mission with the USAF, at the same time I became more and more aware of the importance of this character as a presumed

---

13 Website managed at the time by Don Allis, a gentleman, very interested in the Apollo 20 case.

space exploration insider, the importance of his forecast he disclosed to me, and particularly some sort of increase of celestial phenomena, of which he seemed already knowing the imminent appearance.

Since April 2007 until the summer of the same year, "retiredafb" had already spread on YouTube 13 videos: some of them were contaminated with audio coming from other space missions (Apollo 11 and 15).

In a few weeks some people understood that at least two of them (referred to the so-called video of the "City") are well done fakes, created with official NASA pictures taken by Apollo 17 crew on the Moon (see the chapter V), and audio from the Apollo 15 mission (in this case from one of its EVAs on the Moon).

But nothing of interesting was told and discussed about the footage in which we can see an ingress of some unknown presumed astronauts (apparently without the classic American flag on their spacesuit, on the left sleeve, see the video <<APOLLO 20 TEST Snyder Ingress>>), by some American launching pad. This evidence was often ignored by who believed the entire case to be a big hoax.

And what can we say about the origins of the huge cigar-shaped object that William Rutledge had indicated? Nobody at that time neither could prove that it were not a reality, nor to leave out the tiny possibility of a real artificial object resting on the far side of the Moon. The opinion that the object were a natural rocky formation belonging to the lunar surface – notwithstanding its bizarre form – was accepted almost without doubts.

Moreover, in my opinion nothing of significant was told by the skeptics about the alleged historical facts - not known by the general public – that the controversial insider had provided us in the interview he granted me at the end of May 2007, and even later, on July 1st, 2007: presumed historical facts and small details of Space history that I disclosed in my article <<The Apollo 20 Case: Debunking or a Trojan Horse for the Truth?>>, see the chapter V.

The "Cube" on the far side of the Moon.

Always in that article I wrote for *alienseekernews.com*, I discussed something which came from a sources of mine: an engineer from South America reminded me we must remember the Apollo 13 crew took some amazing pictures of the far side of the Moon: some of them (AS13-60-8608 and AS13-60-8609 images) are very important: they show a strange light reflection coming from our natural satellite. As fact, years ago the famous American researcher Richard Hoagland – former employee at NASA in the media and communication field – had already discussed a particular lunar anomaly of the backside (see www.enterprisemission.com). At the time I expressed the opinion that there could be a connection among the videos of the "City" spread by "retiredafb" on YouTube, and the lunar anomaly discussed by R. Hogland.

I thought that the City indicated by W. Rutledge were just a catalyst to draw media and the public attention, to remember what was already known among the highest levels of NASA and USAF.

Let us see now an excerpt from my old article written in December 2007:

> You can read on the subject an excellent article - <<*Huston, We Have Another Problem*>> - written in 2003 by Steve Troy (www.lunaranomalies.com/houston.htm), in which he uses the expression "Cube" to investigate the two photographs. Troy contacted and worked with Hoagland. Think about to this statement by Steve Troy:
>
> <<<[...] These two photographs proved to be a classibreveal that this area was a veritable "goldmine" of glass artifacts>>
>
> And you might surprise about the location of that lunar anomaly. Why? For two reasons:
>
> 1) William Rutledge never gave us the coordinates of the so-called "City", and the "Cube" is not so far from Tsiolkovsky crater and near Fermi walled plane;
>
> 2) he mentioned the "City" as "station one" in the Apollo 20 schedule (see the interview to William Rutledge, answer nr.17) . So it means that it has a priority for some reasons, or it was just because of its discovery date: made before of the discovery of the cigar-shaped object close to "Izsak D" crater (Apollo 15, 1971).
>
> Moreover, because of a deep knowledge of space flight and of past

space exploration which William Rutledge proved to us, we should keep our mind open about his controversial testimony.

The main reasons which pushed me now to speak out about his revelation on year 2012, are what recently happened in Bangladesh (do you remember the dramatic floods caused last November 2007 by the powerful Cyclone Sidr?) and what is going on in space, since the sudden outburst of the comet P-17 Holmes, at the end of October 2007.

from my article <<*What is Going On in Space? William Rutledge warned me about an Increase of Celestial Phenomena*>>,

by L. Scantamburlo, December 27, 2007

© www.alienseekernews.com; www.angelismarriti.it

From now to year 2012: William Rutledge's forecast

<<*About 2012, i was awared like others, that a major problem could occur during the 2012 year, that some entire countries like Bangladesh and Indonesia, could be flooded. Starting from September 2007, many celestial phenomenons should be visible, it will be increasing till 2012. [...]*>>

July 01, 2007, 01:50 PM, from a "retiredafb's message" to Luca Scantamburlo's YouTube account

Again, it is important to note the strange form of his English. But as I have already explained, in this context do not dwell too much on the mistakes made by Rutledge writing in English (we have already discussed them in the interview). The is also the possibility – that I have never considered in my past articles on Web – that William Rutledge had just made mistakes and grammatical slips on purpose, to give a wrong idea about his identity and his real origin, and the impression he were a hoaxer and a joker.

However, first of all in my opinion we have to pay attention to the date of the message: July 1st, 2007; moreover, we have to pay attention to his warning: he indicated the date of September 2007 as the beginning of an increase of celestial phenomena.

What is going on and has already happened in Space

What happened in Space since September 2007? At that time (of my article) I pointed out some mass media news:

1) at the end of October (between October 23 and 24) because of unknown reasons, the small Comet P-17 Holmes became very bright, changing his brightness by a factor of million, reaching a magnitude of 2.7: it was visible by naked eye (it looked like a star) in the Constellation Perseus, near Cassiopeia, and its sudden outburst is still a mystery for the astronomers; an impact with something from the outer space or just jets of particles from the core?

2) a not well known comet - the Boethin, about a mile in diameter and discovered in 1975 - is suddenly vanished; read about *The New York Times* article:

<<*A Comet Is Missing, So Spacecraft Will Go to NASA's Next Choice*>>

by Henry Fountain, published on December 18, 2007, on *The New York Times*.

The third point I debated, was about an asteroid that could hit Mars in January 2008 (CNN news: <<*Astronomers: Asteroid could hit Mars in January*>>, published on December 21, 2007). Because of these news, I wrote that the Rutledge's testimony about the year 2012 could be connected to what Malachi Martin (1921– 1999) - an eminent theologian and a former Jesuit who worked by the Holy See from 1958 to 1964 - told as guest to the Art Bell radio talk show (the famous *Coast to Coast AM*[14]), in April 1997, during a discussion about the VATT (Vatican Advanced Technology Telescope built in Arizona, on Mount Graham) and his purposes:

<< [...] *Knowledge of what is going on in space and of what is approaching us could be of great import in next 5 - 10 years.*>> said Malachi Martin to Art Bell.

---

14 Art Bell is the creator of *Coast to Coast AM* (now with George Noory, check http://www.coasttocoastam.com), radio talk show in the United States which deals with several topics, but especially with UFOs and paranormal.

The years 2008 and 2009: again outstanding celestial phenomena

But what happened in year 2008 and 2009, went beyond my expectations, giving more credibility to William Rutledge's claims. On October 6, 2008, from the Mt. Lemmon Observatory (Arizona University), some astronomers discovered an asteroid in collision course with the Earth: the name given to it was "Asteroid 2008 TC3", and it was the first time that the astronomical community was able to find out a celestial body before stroke our planet.

The Meteosat-8 satellite – connected to the *European Organisation for the Exploitation of Meteorological Satellites* – was able to take some shoots of this asteroid, which exploded in the atmosphere over Sudan skies. The asteroid came into atmosphere from the outer Space at a speed of 12.8 Km/sec.

In July 2009 a non-professional Australian astronomer by the name of Anthony Wesley (very clever and patient) – during an observation with its telescope - was able to discover signs of a cosmic impact clearly visible in the Jupiter's atmosphere. So, he contacted the major astronomical centers of the world to have a comment, and the astronomical community (NASA included) confirmed that the dark spot on Jupiter was the probable result of an impact on Jupiter of a celestial body: either a comet or an asteroid (consult the NASA article <<*Hubble Space Telescope Rare Jupiter Collision*>>, published in July 2009).

On October 9, 2009, another asteroid exploded in our atmosphere, but over the Indonesia skies. This time its dimensions were greater than the ones of the former asteroid that hit Sudan. An important Italian newspaper – the *Corriere della Sera* (Milan) – dedicated to the celestial phenomenon in Asia an article entitled <<*Un super asteroide fa scattare nel mondo l'allerta anti nucleare*>>[15], by Giovanni Caprara, in which the journalist and science correspondent pointed out the great worry expressed by NASA and USAF specialists. The explosion had a power of 50 kiloton. On the contrary, the asteroid which exploded over Sudan had a power of 1 kiloton.

But the concern of the USAF, about asteroids and comets, should not surprise the reader at this point if we keep in mind what William Rutledge said in 2007. As the matter of fact a few months before the asteroid came into atmosphere over Indonesia, the U.S. Department of

---

15 *Corriere della Sera*, November 2, 2009, page 22.

Defense had already decided to classify the fireballs information and images. In June 2009 *Space.com* published an article by Leonard David, whose title was: <<*Military Hush-Up: Incoming Space Rocks Now Classified*>>.

In the past L. David has been editor-in-chief (or anyway member of the editorial staff) for the magazines *Ad Astra* and *Space World*, so he is an accomplished journalist, and he has been writing for *Space.com* at least for ten years. The DoD decision of classifying the fireballs will prevent the civilian scientists to have access (and to take advantage) to the data and images produced by the U.S. military satellite surveillance network.

In the last 15 years they have had that privilege (a big help for their work).

The Selene "Kaguya", Japanese space probe

To conclude my 2007 website article, I spent a few words on the Japanese space probe named "Kaguya". Since then I thought that William Rutledge - whoever he is, either a former test pilot or an impostor - is a remarkable person who deserves our attention. He seems - because of his statements and forecasts - at the center of a leak of information from the insiders world. I think we should be indebted to him. Let us see again another excerpt from my previous article:

And if we consider the recent baffling declarations by some Japanese politicians[16] - about UFOs and the possible implications of an extraterrestrial visitation or presence on Earth - could not be a mere coincidence. We have to remember that from the Tanegashima Space Center the Japan Aerospace Exploration Agency (JAXA), on September 14 (Japan Standard Time, JST), sent the SELENE "Kaguya" space probe, <<*the most sophisticated lunar exploration mission in the post-Apollo era*>> (from the JAXA documentation, pdf files). In this context SELENE means SELenological & ENgineering Explorer.

Can you imagine what kind of pictures and videos SELENE can get back, from the mysterious far side of the Moon? For sure classified at

16 Consult the articles <<*Defense Minister Ishiba troubled by Legal issues if UFOs arrive*>>, http://www.japantoday.com/jp/news/423193, December 21, 2007; and <<*UFO exist, says Japan official*>>, by Chris Hogg; BBC News, Tokyo, December 2007, http://news.bbc.co.uk/2/hi/asia-pacific/7150156.stm;

the moment. The Japanese politicians who spoke in front of the press about possible extraterrestrial intelligence and UFOs did that as private citizens, but they have showed anyway that at least one country is already ready and enough wise to deal with new challenges for all mankind.

From my article <<*What is Going On in Space? William Rutledge warned me about an Increase of Celestial Phenomena*>>,

by L. Scantamburlo, December 27, 2007

© www.alienseekernews.com; www.angelismarriti.it

That's why in autumn 2009 I wrote an e-mail message to JAXA, a few weeks before my interview with the Italian journalist Sabrina Pieragostini were broadcasted on *Italia 1* channel TV.

I wanted to have an opinion by JAXA on the lunar anomaly I have been investigating and on the possibility to have some highest resolution images (Izsak craters and Fermi walled plane) of the far side of the Moon, taken by Kaguya, photos which do not seem in public domain yet.

But, with my disappointment, I have never received an answer from JAXA. Did they read my message indeed or has it been lost? I do not know, and I cannot verify.

CHAPTER VIII

An Interview With the
Apollo 19 Commander

Revelations by another insider on the Apollo 19/20 case: "moonwalker1966delta" - a YouTube user - claims to be a former NASA astronaut

Introduction

Since May 2007 I have been investigating as freelancer an intriguing case on which so far there is an embarrassing silence in the mass media world: the Apollo 19/20 case, about classified USAF missions - officially never occurred - by NASA assistance and the collaboration of the Soviets.

It seems that up to now only Kevin Smith – see his interview with me in October 2007, during his radio talk The Kevin Smith Show (live from Phoenix, Arizona) has opened a honest discussion on the controversial topic.

Among not many reports on the issue, I want to point out the one written by Steve Johnson for a British bi-monthly publication: <<*The Apollo XX Controversy*>>, pages 31-35, *UFO Data Magazine*, November-December 2007; it is fair and keeps an open mind.

We know the Apollo 19/20 case is a jungle composed by truth and fake; there are contradictory aspects and some misleading data, but at the same time very interesting videos never seen before, official evidence of symmetrical (artificial?) objects resting on the lunar surface, some detailed information on Space exploration and Space flight, and an historical context where to read this astonishing story. My opinion is we are facing some kernels of truth, very important for the mankind's future.

The target of the above-mentioned and presumed military space missions would have been the far side of the Moon, where to explore and collect data about some mysterious and huge objects resting over there; among them, two triangle objects and a huge cigar-shaped object, apparently ancient extraterrestrial space ships.

The insider who - since April 2007 by YouTube - has been telling the story is "retiredafb" (that's his YouTube user name), who claims to be William Rutledge, an American citizen and a former civilian test pilot that would have employed in the last century with Avro, Chance Vought and the USAF, before taking part in Apollo 20 as commander (CDR). The other two crew members of Apollo 20: Leona Marietta Snyder (as CSP) and the famous cosmonaut Alexei Leonov (as LMP).

According to Rutledge's testimony, Apollo 20 was a secret joint US and Soviet space mission that occurred in August 1976 (launch from Vandenberg AFB: August 16), about one year after the famous Apollo-Soyuz Test Project, which launched in July 1975 (Apollo 18 and Soyuz 19).

Kindly at the end of May 2007 "retiredafb" granted me an interview (not by e-mail) by the YouTube General messages service; an interview which I was able to arrange and spread on my website: www.angelismarriti.it; as journalist I thought the story told by "retiredafb" about Apollo 19 and 20 was worthy of attention.

Just to give you an example, an indirect and possible confirmation of the story could be the not well-known ASTP memorial flags signed by Alexei Leonov; P.R[17]. - one Italian citizen who has been following my reports since August 2007 - has found the official link of USSR-AIRSPACE.COM: you can see that the flags look like the mission patch aboard the Constellation, presumed Apollo 20 CSM; even on revver.com another user pointed out the same link.

Rutledge's last job before retiring was working on the KH-11 project (USAF). He explained me also that the ASTP (Apollo-Soyuz Test Project) was the preparatory mission to Apollo 19; and later Apollo 20, after the presumed failure of Apollo 19 and the presumed loss of its crew. Therefore Apollo 20, a classified mission to the Moon alleged by William Rutledge to have taken place aboard a Saturn V moon rocket, would have been preceded by Apollo 19. In recollecting the dramatic loss of the Apollo 19 spacecraft and of its crew, it was an amazing thing to me how William Rutledge was more precise about it before what he told me in the interview (see answer nr.13); on May 23 2007, he told me

---

17 Later the Italian citizen gave me the permission to mention his name: it is Paolo Rosati, quoted even during the special episode of the Italian programme "Mistero" broadcasted on the Italia 1 channel TV, on October 25, 2009.

in our contacts (see Fig.3) that:

<<Apollo 19 had a loss of telemetry wheile being at the end of the TLI, it was not clearly explained at this time, but it is beleived, it was a natural phenomemon, a collision of the aircraft and one of Cruithne brother, who was not identified in 1976. >>

May 23, 2007, 06:12 PM, from my YouTube Account

At the moment William Rutledge (born in Belgium in 1930, in Grembergen, he specified in his user-card on-line on YouTube) moved to another website of files sharing: revver.com, where he has registered himself with the same nickname used on YouTube : "retiredafb". You can see some of his videos at the following address:

http://revver.com/u/retiredafb/

"moonwalker1966delta" speaks out

Later on another YouTube user - by the name of "moonwalker1966delta" - has been beginning to spread alleged classified short videos about Apollo 20 mission. The discussion I present to you in this report is an interview I arranged from questions and answers accomplished by YouTube Account/General Messages. I sent my questions to his account on August 14, 2008, after some contacts by YouTube taken place since May 2008, in which he had already revealed:

1) to be a former NASA astronaut;

2) to be the (survived) Apollo 19 Commander (CMDR), and that *<<since William decided to tell the truth>>*, he thinks *<<it's the right moment to do the same>>*.

Moreover - on July 24, 2008 - in another message he disclosed his alleged identity, with name, surname and his former space missions as astronaut for NASA. I prefer not revealing it - as he has suggested - until more and new elements will be disclosed at last.

If "moonwalker1966delta" has told me the truth about his identity and this will be confirmed, his courageous gesture could change forever the human history and our perspective of humanity's role in the Universe.

The Pentagon, NASA and the Russian Government - in my humble opinion - could take advantage of the revelation: helping to widen mankind horizons in every dimension, both physical and spiritual, and helping to stop the energy crisis, could improve the US and Russia reputations, and to level the current divergences among Moscow and Washington.

As I have already written in a former report, It would be a good thing to disclose and spread the truth about the reality of the extraterrestrial intelligence in the Universe, through an unknown historical fact in which the two great powers of the World of the past (the USA and the USSR) joined together for scientific and peaceful activities, in spite of all their differences and political hostilities.

As pointed out by William Rutledge in one of his comments on YouTube: <<[...] the apollo 20 belongs to all mankind It is a part of all human's heritage>>.

Virgilio wrote: <<Carpent tua poma nepotes>>. The Apollo 20 patch quotes it. Maybe we are those grandchildren...

The interview with "moonwalker1966delta"[18]

- First Part -

In the following interview I have just put the right spaces, and corrected a few orthographic mistakes that there were in our messages (e.g. I have put the right capital letters, like "I" instead of "i", "Earth" instead of "earth", likely written in a hurry, ect.), but I did not change the syntactical construction of the sentences made by "moonwalker1966delta", who - in my opinion - from his English seems an American-English native land, or someone who knows English very well.

1) **Luca Scantamburlo:** *First of all, I want to thank you for your precious time and your kindness. Your YouTube user name is "moonwalker1966delta". In our contacts you did not provide documents which can prove who you are, but you revealed to me your name and surname; you have also declared that you are a former NASA astronaut and you have been "Apollo 19 CMDR", where I know that CMDR, like CDR, means Commander. Of course I have been protecting your identity as I have promised, and I will omit the names of NASA astronauts involved and that you have mentioned, at least for the moment. I wish they will speak out, sooner or later. Can you explain why you have chosen that user name? I think just some clues – if you prefer – could be enough. By the way, last year I received an e-mail about the Apollo 20 case from a former American pilot[19] who wrote:*

<<There is no doubt that the U.S. has been on the moon since 1962 but it did not use rocket propulsion to do this. However rocket launches of Mercury, Gemini and Apollo were used as a cover for

---

18 In the following interview I have just put the right spaces, and corrected a few orthographic mistakes that there were in our messages (e.g. I have put the right capital letters, like "I" instead of "i", "Earth" instead of "earth", likely written in a hurry, ect.), but I did not change the syntactical construction of the sentences made by "moonwalker1966delta", who - in my opinion - from his English seems an American-English native land, or someone who knows English very well. (*original note from the interview, 2008*).

19 This retired American pilot I mention here is John Lear; interested and active in UFO field as revealer, he is also known worldwide because of his friendship wit Bob Lazar. For the fist time I disclose his name here, in this book, as one of my sources and author of the above e-mail I discuss with "moonwalker1966delta". J. Lear has given me his written permission to mention him. He is the son of the famous inventor of the Lear Jet. But John Lear does not seem convinced of the testimony provided by the Apollo 20 insider nicknamed "retiredafb".

the secret program. It is very possible that there were several Apollo launches both before and after the official Apollo program but they would have been launched from Diego Garcia, Kwajalein or Australia (possibly Melville Island) or another secret launch area. A Saturn V launched from Vandenberg although possible seems unlikely because of the size of the rocket and the fact that it was going to the moon. The rotational speed of the earth is significant in all Saturn launches and therefore the launch has to be generally eastbound. Since an eastbound launch out of Vandenberg would be very unlikely [...]>>

Unfortunately I have never received answer from him[20], notwithstanding my several e-mails. That's why I have decided to spread part of his e-mail text. Can you comment on his opinion?

moonwalker1966delta: Dear Luca thank you so much for the opportunity to talk about this matter and all that is related. Honestly I don't know if we have been on the moon since 1962 but I don't agree with it for the simple reason we didn't have the technology to do that and because I followed step by step the lunar missions and the moon era starting from Mercury and Gemini missions to Apollo program and I have never heard about any previous possible mission to the moon.

We launched from Vandenberg Air Force Base and the launch tower and complex has been carried there by sea. One simple assembly building, now shortered[21] for the space shuttle military missions. The LUT tower was same model, the crawler too.

Mission control was located in Yevpatoria for Russia and Vandenberg for USA. To say that launching from Vandenberg for a moon mission would be impossible or quite difficult it's completely wrong and to say that rotational speed of the earth is significant in space launches is also wrong. A classic example could be the launch of Clementine 1 unmanned spacecraft to the moon from Vandenberg Air Force Base on January 25 1994. In reality it is possible to launch a spacecraft to the moon from everywhere on the earth, the only difference would be the longest time and biggest fuel consumption during TLI to insert in the correct trans lunar trajectory. I know that someone used a software to simulate an apollo launch from Vandenberg and the result has been that the first stage and the second stage would have crashed in Arizona

---

20 As I have already discussed in the previous note, at last John Lear answered me giving me his permission to quote his name (e-mail letter dated December 22, 2009).

21 Perhaps here he meant "shortened", instead of "shortered". A probable mistake.

and South Georgia. That is true! But if you take a look at the first stage separation footage of Apollo 11 for example and the Apollo 20 Rutldedge's footage you will notice for sure that the altitude it separated at is much much higher then apollo 11 altitude and the separation speed is much slower and the only reason for it is to make the first and second stage to be yet attracted by earth gravity but enough high to ensure they completely destroy during reentry into the atmosphere.

About my nickname I can say that it represents in only 3 words my inner personal universe and all I have been attracted to. Moonwalker because I walked on the moon. 1966 because during Gemini 10 from 18 to 21 of July 1966 I operated the first computer and delta because it usually indicates a technology resulting from alien technology or generally indicating an alien interference.

2) L.S. *William Rutledge (Apollo 20 CDR) told me that you – crew members of Apollo 19 - were lost in space at the end of TLI maneuver. Since your first answer to my YouTube Account/General Messages – on May 12, 2008 – it touched me on the raw the fact you told me that - in spite of the difficulties - you survived. You said to me:*

> <<I really don't know nor understand why William said we had been lost in space. That's not true. It's true we have been hit by something>>.

And this last thing is what William Rutledge told us. Moreover you affirmed in your first message to me, dated May 12, 2008:

> <<we still don't know what caused a light loss of gyroscopic inertial vector a sudden breakdown of electrical power bus unit and a completely loss of telemetry. We had smoke and light fire on the frontal panel but we have been able to extinguish it at once. As soon as we had electrical power again we stopped manually giroscopic[22] movement. Fortunatly[23] we still have radio contact with Houston and as soon as [name omitted] and [name omitted] entered the simulator we have been able to receive remote telemetry data in voice with [name omitted] and Houston.>>

---

22 The right term is "gyroscopic", with the "y" letter instead of "giroscopic", with the "i". As the matter of fact, above the word is correct. So, just a mistake by the insider using the keyboard.

23 The right term should be "fortunately", instead of "fortunatly".

So – please, correct me if I am wrong - it means that Apollo 19 launching pad was in California and then – after the launch - you were assisted by Houston Mission Control (in Texas), and not by Vandenberg Air Force Base, which is in California?

By the way: on June 24, 2007, I received a message by William Rutledge in which he said to me:

> << Hi Luca, yes i confirm, mission control was in Vandenberg NOT Nasa, it was a political mess, nasa provided the vehicle, it was a russian condition, the vehicle to be a civilian one. Sub contractors helped, except ILC dover , who was not a pure military contractor. Mission control in Vandenberg was slightly different, 5 rooms instead of a big one, little but efficient.>>

Can you comment on it?

moonwalker1966delta: yes that's correct. Mission control for USA was in Vandenberg AFB but we have been forced to use Houston mission control for contingency situation due to incident occurred because the simulator Armstrong and Aldrin used was located at KSC and telemetry link data of the simulator was directly connected to Houston mission control as in usual Apollo Missions. That's why from that moment we used radio and data link with Houston mission control only.

3) L.S. *In your message I mentioned in question nr. 2 of the interview, you said:*

> <<We had to be back up crew of Apollo 19 but since the original crew has been cancelled about 3 weeks before launch we became the mission crew while [name omitted] and [name omitted] have been selected as back up crew. [...] we haven't got women on board but another official Apollo program astronaut as pilot and another russian cosmonaut with exceptional medical skills.>>

What can you tell me about Stephanie Ellis (Abidjan, Ivory Coast, 1946 - ? 1976)? Was she a member of the Apollo 19 original crew, later on cancelled? And can you confirm the identity of the Soviet cosmonaut scheduled for Apollo 19? William Rutledge told me he was "Aleksei Sorokin" (YouTube message received by me on July 15, 2007). I spread this information to the public for the first time. What happened to them?

moonwalker1966delta: Yes I confirm original Apollo 19 crew members were Stephanie Ellis Aleksei Sorokin and John Swigert. John died in 1982 for cancer but Stephanie and Aleksei disappeared in 1975 and 1976. I don't know the real reason they have been removed from Apollo 19 crew but someone said Stephanie was talking around too much about Apollo 19 mission and the moon spacecraft. I heard she died at the end of 1975 during a training flight.

4) L.S. *Have you ever met Leona Marietta Snyder, Apollo 20 CSP?*

moonwalker1966delta: Yes I met Leona Snyder and William 2 months after Apollo 20 reentry during a secret conference at KSC and again in 1993 at a restaurant in San Antonio with Leonov and David Scott.

5) L.S. *Can you tell me when and where - if it happened - did you meet William Rutledge for the first and the last time?*

moonwalker1966delta: The first time I met William was in 1974 at JSP where I have been selected as chief of astronauts. I was training for Apollo 19 and when I knew the names of Apollo 20 crew I ask to meet him and I have been very impressed about his knowledge of alien technology we are working about at that time. The last time has been in San Antonio in 1993.

[...]

The end of the first part of the interview

© Luca Scantamburlo

freelance writer member of the Free Lance International Press

September 15, 2008

www.angelismarriti.it

Apollo 20: for the Soviets the Mission Control was in Yevpatoriya. The revelations by "moonwalker1966delta" confirm Rutledge's testimony

In one of his first messages sent to me, William Rutledge (aka "retiredafb") told me that for the Soviets the Apollo 20 mission control was in Yevpatoriya. "moonwalker1966delta" has confirmed this detail (above, see his answer to question nr. 1).

Here you are - spread to the general public - part of a Rutledge's message, never revealed before by me:

> <<[...] Russians had another mission control in Yevpatoria, Lyosha could take his orders from there , anyway there was no interference between russians and US military. I saw your note about medals... We were fired out any space program. The american space program fell abruptly after Jimmy carter's election. Gerald Ford was a big fan of space program, cooperation between CCCP and USA was very active, he had clear views about the space shuttle program. In august 1976, he was busy about elections and didn't participated or watched any part of the adventure.>>

"retiredafb" on YouTube - in a message[24] to Luca Scantamburlo (YouTube Account/General Messages, June 24, 2007), the same message mentioned in my question nr. 2 of the interview to "moonwalker1966delta".

In May 2007 - at the beginning of our contacts - William Rutledge wrote to me about two other towns:

> <<[...] i'm forced to use a anonymizer program. I'm still very carefull , and i wish, if it is ok for you, to reply on this youtube adress.
>
> You can ask me everythig , i'll just have to give the names of employees of the lower class, other names will not be a problem.>>

> <<[...] the chief of the russian programm was in the Ural, in the towns of Nijni Tagil and Sverdlovsk (today Yekaterinburg).>>

"retiredafb" on YouTube - in a message to Luca Scantamburlo (YouTube Account/General Messages, May 18, 2007).

© Luca Scantamburlo

freelance writer member of the Free Lance Internationl Press, September 15, 2008, www.angelismarriti.it

---

24 As I use to do, the written messages by retiredafb are here presented without any correction (e.g. American rather than "american", or I rather than "i"), on the contrary of the interview with him I edited at the end of May 2007, that I had presented revised.

The interview with "moonwalker1966delta"

- Second Part -

8) L.S. *What can you tell me about Charles Peter Conrad and James Irwin as CapCom? Moreover, have you ever met prof. Valentin Alexeiev, mentioned by W. Rutledge as the presumed person in charge of the mission in Soviet Union, and who would have become later on the President of the Academy of Science in Urals?*

moonwalker1966delta: Yes I can confirm Charles Peter Conrad[25] and James Irwin as CAPCOM of Apollo 20 and no I have never personally met Alexeiev though he has been the Soviet Mission Director for my mission too.

10) L.S. *What were your mission targets, as Apollo 19 crew?*

moonwalker1966delta: Our main targets were one of the triangular object located south of the main mothership, the mothership herself and the moon base located SW of the mothership. Our landing site was the same of Apollo 20. Soviets launched the SL-12 2 months before our mission and Luna 21 landed on the west side of the crater. Apollo 20 used Lunokhod 2 as a radio beacon to land exactly on the second largest rockstair not far from Luna 21. Rutledge and Leonov made and extensive use of Lunokhod 2 due to it's highly sophisticated equipment necessary for this kind of mission not only the 4 panoramic telephotometers but also the X-ray scope combined with laser telemeter and the radiation detector to verify the possible radiations emitted by the ship and the base.

11) L.S. *What can you tell me about the origin of the alien spacecrafts resting on the backside of the Moon: the cigar-shaped object and the two triangles? Is there any relationship among them? And can you give me once again – as you have already done in a private message - the lunar coordinates of the triangle objects, never revealed before?*

moonwalker1966delta: The origin of the two objects the mothership and the alien base were the same. Same materials and same age. We think they have been shot down during a sort of "lunar Pearl Harbor".

---

25 The correct name is "Charles Pete Conrad", not Peter, as I have already written in another footnote.

The base has been completely destroyed and the mothership and the 2 spacecraft shot down during and emergency take off. That is what William and Leonov thought too. As I previously answered in our private message the 2 objects are clearly visible in AS15-P-9625 and AS15-P-9630 in the upper side of the pic and just right of the mothership at coordinates 18.7S - 116.92E and 18.31S - 117.48E. You can notice they are absolutly identical in their triangular shape. If you use a software like NASA World Wind it could be easy to locate them and notice the green metallic brilliance of the first object.

12) L.S. *Lunar coordinates of the presumed alien space mothership: Nose 17.3 deg S, 117.62 deg E; Cockpit 17.15 deg S, 117.62 deg E; Base 17.20 deg S, 117.62 deg E. Were they given us inverted? The longitude is coherent with the position of the huge object (approximately 4 km long). The problem is with the latitude: not with the latitude data, but with their reference to the major parts of the object (the nose and the base). We should have their reversal, in my opinion. What do you think?*

moonwalker1966delta: We had to do the same footage and follow the same path. If you follow the path of the LM in the first part of the footage and compare it on a lunar map you will see that is coherent with the subtitles and the camera we had to use would have been a 16mm Maurer motion picture cameras with 10mm lenses with the Data Acquisition Camera Mount connected to the the window sliding rail through a knob. In the second part of the video the footage is provided by mounting a photolens of 75 mm with it's aperture aligned to the LM X axis + 1 degree and usually used to film the outdoor CM manouvers and alignments. In this second part of the footage the trajectory is not coherent to the previous trajectory nor to the subtitles. I think the second part has been inverted and the subtitles followed the inverted images providing the right coordinates but in the opposite sequence. The video must be seen reverted from the bottom to the cockpit and the subtitles indications must be reverted too leaving the coordinates data unchanged. That's my idea.

[...]

The end of the second part

© Luca Scantamburlo, freelance writer member of the Free Lance International Press, October 11, 2008

August 2008, another whistleblower speaks out: "Anonymous ATS"

Weeks ago I had an e-mail contact with Bill Ryan (Project Camelot) concerning the Apollo 20 case and William Rutledge's footage, especially the footage about the EBE "Mona Lisa" spread by "retiredafb" on revver.com.

B. Ryan told me that many people think the footage is a fake but - at the same time - he pointed out a very interesting topic on AboveTopSecret (ATS) forum, where last August an anonymous individual wrote something that I should have read it.

The title of the topic is "Apollo 20 update", begun in April 2008. The remarkable intervention is the one posted at 09:50 PM on August 14, 2008, by "Anonymous ATS".

source: http://abovetopsecret.com/forum/thread347845/pg11

The whistleblower is - according to the written testimony - the son of a former NRO employee who years ago - before to die because of an "inoperable cancer" – revealed a secret which has always been a weight on his chest: to have participated, as member of a Mission control team, to <<[...] an ultra-black project in the mid-70's that sent another mission to the moon to investigate a particularly provacative anomaly>>.

NRO (National Reconnaissance Office) is a very important intelligence agency, and "Anonymous ATS" is right when he says <<[...] It was declassified in 1992...>>.

Well, there are some details told by this whistleblower very close to the aspects of Rutledge's story: same year (1976) in which the black operation would have been occurred, same location for the Mission Control (Vandenberg AFB) and same goal: investigating a lunar singularity, which in 1973 <<[...] was confirmed>> as <<[...] in fact a derelict spacecraft>>.

There are also some inconsistencies: for example a different position from where to launch the spacecraft - not Vandenberg but an island in the Indian Ocean - and no signs of triangular objects and no extraterrestrial creatures recovered.

But the whistleblower told us also that <<[...] My father said that the *project was highly compartmentalized so he did not know the whole story>>.*

[...]

© Luca Scantamburlo

freelance writer member of the Free Lance International Press

October 11, 2008

www.angelismarriti.it

Inside the Constellation (Apollo 20 spacecraft, August 1976). Frames (original colours deleted) from the <<*APOLLO 20 ALIEN SPACESHIP ON THE MOON CSM FLYOVER*>>: a presumed 16 mm footage taken by Leona M. Snyder; source: YouTube, added by "retiredafb" on June 24, 2007.

Image credit: "retiredafb", YouTube;

reproduction by kind permission of "retiredafb" (William Rutledge)

Frame from a video added on April 8, 2008, by "retiredafb" on revver.com: likely the man is William Rutledge, the Apollo 20 CDR, here aboard the Lunar Module Phoenix (LM-15) on the far side of the Moon (August 1976);

video <<*Apollo 20 E.B.E. MonaLisa TV unscheduled transmission*>>, MET 174, unscheduled TV transmission

Image credit: "retiredafb", Revver;

reproduction by kind permission of "retiredafb" (William Rutledge)

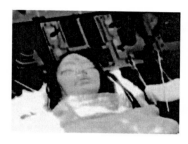 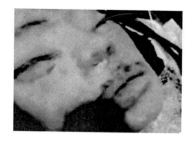

Frames (original colours deleted) from a presumed unscheduled TV transmission: the so-called "EBE Mona Lisa" aboard the Phoenix LM-15 (Apollo 20, MET 174), found - according to the insider "retiredafb" - aboard another derelict spacecraft (but triangular) resting on the far side of the Moon, probably not too far from the cigar-shaped object (the mothership), and brought to earth by the LEM crew of Apollo 20. You can observe a shadow on the EBE's face; during the video the shadow moves; does it mean is there someone in front of her and is he shooting both the EBE and William Rutledge indeed?

Video <<*Apollo 20 E.B.E. MonaLisa TV unscheduled transmission*>> added on April 8, 2008, by "retiredafb" on revver.com

Image credit: "retiredafb", Revver;

reproduction by kind permission of "retiredafb" (William Rutledge)

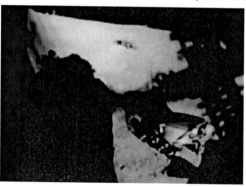

Presumed lunar surface through a LM-15 (Apollo 20 LEM) window: frame from the same video discussed above; the lander on the surface looks like a Soviet Lunokhod. See the answer nr. 10 of my interview with "moonwalker1966delta", for further explanations.

Image credit: "retiredafb", Revver;

reproduction by kind permission of "retiredafb" (William Rutledge)

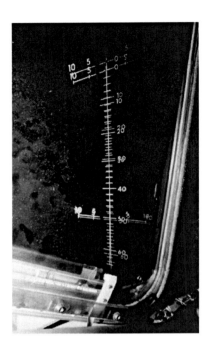

The Landing Point Designator (L.P.D.) on a LEM window.

Image credit: NASA Photo

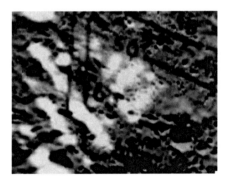

Frame from the video <<*ALIEN SPACESHIP ON THE MOON flyover bef. landing APOLLO 20*>> spread on YouTube by "retiredafb" on May 4, 2007. You can notice numbers visible in the frame, coherent with the presence of a L.P.D. on the LEM window.

Image credit: "retiredafb", YouTube

reproduction by kind permission of "retiredafb" (William Rutledge)

Detail from the AS17-M-2613 photo; Lens Focal Length: 3 inch, Camera Tilt: VERT,
Camera Altitude: 113 km, Sun Elevation: 24°, (Apollo Image Atlas)
Image credit: The Lunar and Planetary Institute (LPI) – NASA Photo

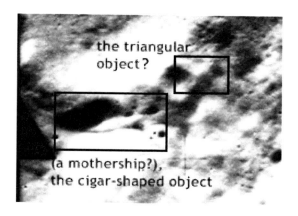

Same detail reproduced above, but changed in contrast and brightness by the Author
(L.S.) to point out the lunar anomalies.

105

CHAPTER IX

Moon: An Ultra Black Operation To Investigate a "Derelict Spacecraft"?

In this chapter I discuss the main points made by the Anonymous ATS, about his father's story. About the original text – that I do not reproduce here, with exception of a few words embodied in quotation marks - I invite you to consult the AboveTopSecret website and the topic "Apollo 20 update"[26]. Here I just summarize the anonymous testimony to the best of my comprehension.

1. According to the story, his father (this presumed former NRO employee discussed in the AboveTopSecret forum, and who would have disclosed a hidden truth while was on the point of death with his son) did not mention any sort of "Apollo 20", or anything connected to Apollo ghost missions, and he has never even given any official name to the mission. Other details were that there were no markings either on the rocket or on the spacecraft. This special mission was completely "off the books". No one involved in such an operation used his/her real name.

2. Mission Control was located at Vandenberg AFB. On the contrary, the launch operation center was located on Diego Garcia Island, in the Indian Ocean, along the equator, because this site was the ideal place to launch Eastwards, with almost nothing around the space launch complex (only water).

3. The US President Nixon was the person who initiated the operations, through his orders issued in late 1971. The work of Anonymous ATS's father, began in 1974 but the secret space manned lunar mission took place in 1976. The father told his son that he submitted to *<<an intensive psychological exam before he was selected to join the program>>*. He told him that he was chosen – among the other things – because he was a reliable

---

26 *<<Apollo 20 update>>*, Topic started on 9-4-2008, 09:33 AM by JohnnyRaincheck reply posted on 14-8-2008, 09:50 PM by Anonymous ATS, source: http://abovetopsecret.com/forum/thread347845/pg11. Anoymous ATS is a member of AboveTopSecret.com, a debate board community of Internet.

person.

4. The special mission consisted of 3 American astronauts, whose names are unknown to his son, because his father did not mention them. The father told him also that the special training for these men lasted nearly 4 years. And it was in 1973 that without doubts the Authorities - involved in such a concealed mission - knew that the resting object on the Moon <<*was in fact a derelict spacecraft*>>. The father had the possibility to review personally the images of this spacecraft.

5. This spaceship <<*was speculated to be roughly 1.5 million years old*>>, but he could not examine all the information; but some of them said that the spacecraft was damaged because of old meteor impacts, and because of an "ancient crash". About its form, it was a cigar-shaped object with a section approximately of 1 mile. Evidence collected, seemed to indicate that it had already been explored before the human expedition took place. About possible alien remains, the result was negative. About the artificial material, 300kg of this material was brought back to earth by astronauts. The former NRO employee described to his son what he <<*called "strange hieroglyphs and markings" covering what was assumed to be the the the "cockpit" of the craft.*>>

6. Not only the US were involved in such a secret operation: at least 2 other governments took a part in this black project. Interesting another detail reported to his son: the father remembered that a British analyst worked with him, and moreover he knew about a smaller team in Australia, although he thought the Australian government were not completely aware of what they were doing.

Old and new considerations on the Anonymous ATS whistleblower

As I have already written in my article entitled <<*August 2008, another wistleblower speaks out*>> - see my interview with "moonwalker1966delta" - there are some points that are coherent with the story and with the Rutledge's testimony. About point nr. 3, as the matter of fact the following year - in May 1972 - the U.S. President Richard Nixon and the Soviet politician Kosygin - in spite of the Cold War times - signed in Moscow an important agreement on Space and technology: a five years agreement of cooperation among the United States and Soviet Union: <<*Agreement Concerning Cooperation in the Exploration and Use of Outer Space for Peaceful Purposes.*>> That's why the

Apollo-Soyuz Test Project (ASTP) was possible, in July 1975.

But most important it is the fact that some of the details of this presumed and unknown piece of XX Century history, are coherent with some aspects told me by William Rutledge (the alleged Apollo 20 CDR) by YouTube messages, but aspects I revealed to the general public only with that article spread on my website at the end of October 2008, after the testimony by "Anonymous ATS". In that occasion I posted some snapshots of our contacts as evidence.

For example the "Anonymous ATS" has written: <<[...] *there were no markings on the rocket or spacecraft*>>.

On June 6, 2007, I received a message by William Rutledge in which he told me that:

> <<[...] *On the lift off sequence, the saturn 5 has no markings till the third stage. [...] In vandenberg, the saturn V launch had to be not reconizable, no BW lines or USA marks on the rocket. Only the last ring was black painted, and it could look like an ordinary Delta rocket at 4 miles distance.*>>[27].

from Luca Scantamburlo's YouTube account, message by "retiredafb" (received on June 6, 2007, 01:37 AM)

Moreover, "Anonymous ATS" had reported in his point nr. 6 about at least two other Governments involved in the classified project. What it is interesting, is that on May 23, 2007, 06:12 AM (at the beginning of our contacts) I received a YouTube message by William Rutledge where he wrote me that:

> <<[...] *about nation involved*
>
> *1 As far as i know, it's USA and Russia, but i would not be surprised if france is on this program, MHD*[28] *and anti matter is used in this country.*>>

from Luca Scantamburlo's YouTube account, message by "retiredafb" (received on May 23, 2007, 06:12 AM)

---

27 As usual, the "retiredafb"'s message is here reproduced in its original form, without any correction by me.

28 MHD means "MagnetoHydroDynamics", a revolutionary technology to further increase the hypersonic speed of an aircraft. On this basis, was conceived and designed the generator of Ajax, the secret Russian aircraft (an Hypersonic Aircraft Concept). The Ajax is the aircraft mentioned by William Rutledge in my interview with him (see his answer to question nr. 4, chapter I).

And at 09:26 am on July 15, 2007, I received a message by William Rutledge where he wrote that:

> <<[...] I'd like to post the genuine sound but they are on separated tapes. Many people , radio amateur were tracking the apollo missions , so the sound was coded and was separated from video , secrecy was kept unless i think than French and British got the tv feeds (m' not sure of this).>>

from Luca Scantamburlo's YouTube account, message by "retiredafb" (received on July 15, 2007, 09:26 AM)

Another coherent aspect of the new testimony

Moreover, the Anonymous ATS remembers his father told him that the crew chosen for the ultra secret manned mission towards the dark side of the Moon, was trained for nearly 4 years (see point nr. 4 of the first paragraph of the chapter), and as the matter of fact the insider "moonwalker1966delta" - in his answer nr. 5 of the first part of my interview with him - tells me that he met William Rutledge in 1974, and at the time he ("moonwalker1966delta") was already training for Apollo 19 mission. Pretty coherent with the other information disclosed by "Anonymous ATS", who placed the mission date in the year 1976.

The derelict spacecraft already explored by others?

Another thing coherent with the disclosure by "Anonymous ATS", is the detail about a previous exploration made by someone else, before the human expedition occurred (see point nr. 5). If you remember the retiredafb's user-card on-line on YouTube, posted on April 1, 2007, it said: <<[...] Note that the ship has already been explored before the first human expedition reached the lunar singularity.>>

Some hyphotheses on the whistleblowers: a big hoax or genuine insiders involved in a disclosure?

So, this means that if the Apollo 19/20 case is a big hoax - but anyway on the basis of bizarre details visible on official Apollo photos, taken by NASA astronauts during Apollo 15 and 17 missions - one person or a team of very mysterious individuals is doing a very difficult and strange job: many pieces of information, spread on Web at a distance of more than 1 year and only by Internet means, fit into each other like pieces of a big puzzle but in which there are also missing parts and strong contradictions that seem unjustified and inexplicable.

Unless we are in the presence of more genuine witnesses, separate from each other, and that they have decided independently to disclose a truth which changed their life. But is it possible?

In the case of a real disclosure with contradictions and misleading data provided to the general public, it is likely that someone - at some Government level - has taken a decision to allow an unofficial and partial disclosure carried out in a controversial way. And it is possible that, after the first disclosure by "retiredafb" since April 2007, others involved in Apollo 19 and 20 missions have really decided to follow his steps as anonymous insiders, but they do not know the story in all its details and aspects. The "Anonymous ATS" – as near relative of one them - could be one an indirect witness, in possession of second-hand information.

On the contrary, "moonwalker1966delta" seems now – a part from the beginning in which he was surprised by his fellow astronaut's actions on YouTube – fully involved in the disclosure and in contact with William Rutledge. About this possibility, there is not only the fact I have got the permission to use retireafb's footage to illustrate my book, just by "moonwalker1966delta" who informed me I have had his permission (at the end of December 2009, through my YouTube Account/General Messages), but also through an evidence of a detail included in an old message by "retiredafb" himself, dated June 6, 2007, and that I will discuss later, in the chapter XIII.

A detail on which I have never thought too much in 2007 and 2008. But, as the history teaches, the small details are always very important.

CHAPTER X

Apollo 19:
The Radio Dialogue

Apollo 19? Why not, if Apollo 18 did take place (ASTP)

In the past I wrote an article for my website in which I reminded that there is an official NASA Web page with an indication that Apollo-Soyuz Test Project (the ASTP) was a mission involving Soyuz 19 and Apollo 18 capsules; that page can be found at the following link:

http://www.hq.nasa.gov/office/pao/History/apollo/welcome.html

The caption "Apollo 18" identifies who the United States crew members of the ASTP were: Thomas P. Stafford, Vance D. Brand, Donald K. "Deke" Slayton. Although we have no evidence in the historical record that Apollo 18 was followed by Apollo 19 (due to Apollo 19 being most a secret USAF mission, with NASA collaboration), William Rutledge gave a precise definition for the ASTP. It was correct, in spite of the fact this information is not well-known by the general public.

To whom it may concern, and to all the readers of my website, I remind that after the "retiredafb" testimony, another whistleblower of the controversial Apollo 19-20 case has come out: the alleged Apollo 19 Commander, a former NASA astronaut who revealed his name to me, through our contacts. I was not able to check his credentials, but the amount and the nature of the footage he spread on Internet, are quite interesting. On Youtube his nickname is "moonwalker1966delta".

The interview who granted to me, in year 2008, is rich in details and helped me to find out one of the two huge triangular objects resting on the far side of the Moon, and mentioned by William Rutledge in my interview with him (year 2007); the mysterious triangular object is near the cigar-shaped object.

Apollo 19 incident and what happened in 1976

"Moonwalker1966delta" - on November 09, 2008 - posted on YouTube an outstanding video of Apollo 19 secret space mission: taken probably by chance inside the Lunar Module (and this could explain why we do not see any astronaut in the video; but I am not sure about it[29]), after the TLI, the so-called Trans Lunar Injection maneuver; the TLI is the acronym used to indicate the propulsion maneuver which sets a spacecraft on a trajectory which will intersect the Moon.

On YouTube "moonwalker1966delta" had commented the video with the following words:

> "Apollo 19 just hit by something and loosing telemetry data.Fire and smoke on AC-BC cell bus and aborting mission after TLI insertion".

But what can we say about the radio dialogue?

First of all we have to say something about the presumed incident occurred to Apollo 19 mission: according to Apollo 19 Commander, there was a <<*a light loss of gyroscopic inertial vector a sudden breakdown of electrical power bus unit and a completely loss of telemetry.*>>

The crew had <<*smoke and light fire on the frontal panel*>> but they have been able to estinguish it very soon. Once they had electrical power again, they stopped the giroscopic movement. Then, they got help from Houston where a couple of astronauts entered the simulator. It was not very clear to me where the Mission Control was.

So "moonwalker1966delta" - in the answer nr. 2 of my interview with him - said to me:

> <<*Mission control for USA was in Vandenberg AFB but we have been forced to use Houston mission control for contingency situation due to incident occured[30] because the simulator [...]" - [names omitted] - "used was located at KSC and telemetry link data of the simulator was directly connected to Houston mission control as in usual Apollo Missions. That's why from that moment we used radio and data link with Houston mission control only.*>>

---

29 As the matter of fact, one of my sources - "a Chinese" - has pointed out to me by e-mail that in the footage of the incident there are recognizable details of the Command Module. So, the Apollo 19 incident footage would show the interior of a CSM (the Constellation, Apollo 20 CSM in this case).

30 The right word is "occurred", not "occured".

So, some NASA astronauts of backup crew would have helped Apollo 19 crew to survive and come back to earth. Now we have to remember that even the other whistleblower - "retiredafb", the alleged William Rutledge, Apollo 20 Commander - in recollecting the dramatic loss of the Apollo 19 spacecraft and its crew, was precise about it before what he told me in the interview (see answer nr.13); on May 23, 2007, he told me in our contacts (see Fig.2) that:

> <<Apollo 19 had a loss of telemetry wheile being at the end of the TLI, it was not clearly explained at this time, but it is beleived, it was a natural phenomemon, a collision of the aircraft and one of Cruithne brother, who was not identified in 1976.>>[31]

May 23, 2007, 06:12 PM, from Luca Scantamburlo's YouTube Account.

But we now know - according to "moonwalker1966delta", Apollo 19 Commander - that William Rutledge (a.k.a "retiredafb") told us something wrong - perhaps on purpose in my opinion - to drive someone else to tell the truth. Apollo 19 crew had the incident, but it survived.

Apollo 19: the radio dialogue and its transcription

Recently I have been in contact with a kind American citizen who has helped me to have an accurate transcription of the dramatic radio dialogue among the presumed Apollo 19 crew and the Mission Control on the ground. Mr. W. - a gentleman who prefers to stay behind the scenes - gave me weeks ago what he believes to be a good transcription of that conversation. He is 90% sure that is what they said. You can compare the text I present to you, with original voices, listening to the video posted on YouTube by "moonwalker1966delta", at the following link:

http://www.youtube.com/watch?v=MQMTbsePb7Q

Here you are the text, almost a complete transcription of the radio dialogue; some words are not understandable because of the bad quality of the audio (I have coupled every statement to what I believe

---

31 As I use to do, the written messages by retiredafb are here presented without any correction (e.g. It would be "while" instead of "wheile", and "phenomenon" instead of "phenomemon"), on the contrary of the interview with him I edited at the end of May 2007, and that I had presented revised.

the right person; I have identified at least three different voices during the radio dialogue, the I have called: "Mission Control or Astronaut", the first voice; "Astronaut?", the second voice; and "Mission Control", the third voice):

> Mission Control or Astronaut (1st voice): *"Flight Go to CMF 2 SPS check SL 2 show high temp. reading [...] shows negative SPS power check indicators."*

> Mission Control or Astronaut (1st voice): *"Okay [...] confirm that cell shut down commence emergency power down procedure."*

> Mission Control or Astronaut (1st voice): *"Here's the check CSM 2 SPS data in the inverter we might have an explosive fuel cell problem. Stand by to shut down all fuel cells!"*

> [sound of explosion]

> Mission Control or Astronaut (1st voice): *"Telemetry shows unusual battery one and two drain and low fuel [...] Stand by!"*

> Astronaut? (2nd voice): *"Abort!"*

> Mission Control (3rd voice): *"This is Apollo Center Launch Control, we have an emergency situation. Mission's aborted."*

> Mission Control or Astronaut (1st voice): *"Mission aborted. Stand by for data".*

Transcription of the dialogue made by Mr. W.

Thanks to his kindness.

© L. Scantamburlo

September 23, 2009

www.angelismarriti.it

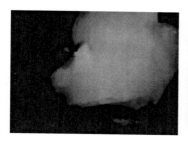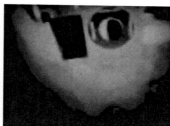
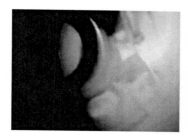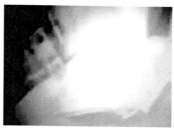

Several frames (b/w, without the original colours, here deleted) from the video
<<*Apollo 19 incident*>>, uploaded on November 9, 2008, on YouTube by
"moonwalker1966delta", the alleged Apollo 19 Commander: it would be an evidence (16
mm footage he told me in my previous contacts) of the Apollo 19 incident, taken place
at the end of TLI.

Comment added by the Apollo 19 Commander:

<<*Apollo 19 just hit by something and loosing telemetry data.Fire and smoke on AC-BC
cell bus and aborting mission after TLI insertion*>>

(February 1976?)

Image credit: "moonwalker1966delta", YouTube;

reproduction by kind permission of "moonwalker1966delta"

PART II

FURTHER INVESTIGATIONS

CHAPTER XI

The Reasons
For the Disclosure

In my written interview with William Rutledge, I ask him the reasons why he decided to speak out (read his answer nr.6, Chapter I). William Rutledge had already told me something in our previous contacts through my YouTube account.

Let us see an excerpt from them:

> [...] I choosed to to it know because all apollo program had to be definitely locked with th outgoing of 'the marvel of it all' presented april 20, presenting the 12 astronauts alive who stayed on the moon.
>
> I t was a trahison for me , for alexei, and for the 3 dead astronauts of amollo 19. My girlfriend Stephanie ELlis, first american woman in sace, fisrt afro maerican woman was killed during this mission, i have no place topray for her, her remains are still in orbit around earth.>>

May 23, 2007, 07:48 AM, from a retiredafb's message to my YouTube account

So, W. Rutledge told me he began disclosing the Apollo 19 and 20 story because of *The Wonder Of It All*[32], a film by Jeffrey Roth that would be like a sort of "trahison" for him and the other astronauts sent by secrecy to the dark side of the Moon.

We had already read this message by him (with many mistakes in his English form). First of all, we can notice that he says: *'the marvel of it all'*, which is not correct, because the exact title is *The Wonder Of It All*, and in fact in the interview with him, his answer is correct in naming it again (read answer nr. 6) This means that his mistake was just a so-called lapsus calami.

---

32 [...] 6) L.S. *When and above all why did you decide to disclose these information about classified space missions and is there anybody who is protecting you?*

W.R.   It's the announcement of "the wonder of it all" maybe, and 2012 is coming fast. I also think that UFOs will appear more often starting from September 2007. A lot of people died around me in Rwanda, and I have more time to take care of this. About protection, please understand it's hard to speak of my armoury. [...] *From my interview with him, see Chapter I;*

And as I have already written in the chapter I, the video trailer of the film - in his written notes - says: <<*Only 12 Men Have Ever Walked On the Moon*>>.

Only 12 men? This is what the official Space history tells. Therefore, if William Rutledge is really a former astronaut and test pilot, employed by the USAF as the Apollo 20 Commander, we can understand all his great disappointment with that statement about "only 12 men" as moonwalkers.

Of course I am sure in this case Jeffrey Roth – who has done an excellent job with his film – is not responsible for possible missing parts of space history, owing to their feature of their secrecy: secret space mission which are socially and economically disruptive if disclosed, as *SpaceHeroes.org* pointed out years ago.

Second point: the use of a French expression like "trahison" - which means "betrayal" - does not seem a sign of an American-English native land. It is consistent with the story he told me about him, and his presumed residence in Rwanda. This point does not mean he told us the truth about his identity, of course.

Third point: let us examine the date he has mentioned: April 20 (2007 of course). I wrote about it even on the pages of the report-interview published on a bi-monthly Italian magazine, for which I was a collaborator: *UFO Notiziario*[33].

At the time I could not find any reference to this date. And in Italy the first news I could read about the coming out of the film by Jeffrey Roth, was in a newspaper article entitled <<*Voci dal viaggio più lungo*>>, published by *La Stampa* (Turin, Italy) on June 27, 2007, at the bottom of the page I of its enclosed file *TuttoScienze*. In the article the author mentioned that the documentary by Jeffrey Roth was showed to a selected public of scientists and technicians at the Kennedy Space Center (KSC, NASA) in Florida, three weeks before.

So, I thought that "retiredafb" - who claims to be William Rutledge – had to be well-informed about Space history and its celebration initiatives in USA. Three weeks before June 27, 2007, means the first days of June, not the end of April. So, I was very surprised.

---

[33]   <<*Apollo 20, Agosto 1976: Missione segreta USA-URSS sulla Luna? Intervista con William Rutledge, presunto CDR dell'equipaggio Apollo 20*>> , by Luca Scantamburlo, *UFO Notiziario*, nr. 70, August-September 2007, pag. 46.

Was it possible that the film had already been showed even before, somewhere else? But it seemed that only William Rutledge knew something about it. I did not anything.

Only a couple of years later I found the reference to *The Wonder Of It All* actually showed on April 20, 2007, during an official presentation of the film at the Newport Beach Film Festival in California, with former NASA astronauts as special guests[34]. And I also realized that the day after the date mentioned by Rutledge (i.e. April 21, 2007), the retired NASA astronaut John W. Young spoke to the public, at the Radisson Newport Beach Hotel, with his lecture whose title was *Preservation and Survival: Space Exploration and Earth's Future*[35].

The question is: why I was not able to find any reference to the date of April 20, 2007, at the time, but I was able years later? I cannot answer with certainty. One possibility is I did not search very well (it could be, but I do not think so). Another one is that the Web search engine I used, did not work as I expected because the news was released noiselessly.

One more consideration: let's think over what he told me at the end of May 2007 (the reason for disclosure was the film), and about the date of the first video uploaded on YouTube: April 1st, 2007. The other videos posted on YouTube in April, were on April 4, 5, 7, and on April 9, 2007.

This means that before that film was officially presented to the general public - at the Newport Beach Film Festival - William Rutledge had already a project, very clear in his mind or ready to be changed.

If all the story is a big hoax, anyone can easily understand that he also made a very suitable choice: choosing the date of April 20, 2007 and its celebration as the main justification for his disclosure, does not make too much sense because he began the disclosure before April 20, 2007. But it proves he was fully aware of what was going on in the Space community, and above all of its celebrations. Did he give us a clue about his identity, to prove he is a retired military insider indeed? Again, something seems wrong: he claimed to be – in his comments on YouTube – a "Civilian Former test pilot on various aircrafts"[36]. But he

---

34 http://www.collectspace.com/ubb/Forum2/HTML/000026.html

CollectSPACE was – in this occasion - a partner with the Newport Beach Film Festival.

35 http://newportbeachfilmfestival.blogspot.com/
http://www.collectspace.com/ubb/Forum2/HTML/000026.html

36 From retiredafb's YouTube profile.

told me he was employed by the military, and that the USAF employed him, because he was a volunteer for the MOL-Gemini Project (he was not chosen at the time, he revealed to me in a message).

Does it make any sense for the USAF to choose a civilian pilot for such a dangerous and secret mission to the Moon? It is obvious that if William Rutledge did fly to the dark side of the Moon as Apollo 20 Commander, he was a military test pilot, not just a simple civilian test pilot. Unless we do not think to the expression he used on his YouTube profile, with the following meaning: a former test pilot, who is now just a civilian (because he is a an ex pilot, and a retired officer from the military; in fact almost all the former test pilots in USA involved in space missions were and are military officers, retired or still on duty). However the expression he used is ambiguous, and probably on purpose.

Moreover, how can we explain his choice to give credibility to an outstanding and unbelievable story of secret space missions with the reference to a film-documentary just released, and at the same time spreading contradictory information? Think for example to all the mistakes made by him in his English form, the story of his presumed residence in Rwanda, the strange subtitles of the radio dialogue made by other people (his friends?) and posted on the LEM flyover footage (see Appendix III), ect.

On the contrary, if there are kernels of truth behind his testimony, is obvious that William Rutledge – as former test pilot and secret moonwalker of a hidden Space history – could take advantage of *The Wonder of It All* official presentation, and knowing its coming release even in advance. That's why he had already projected the disclosure, that started before April 20, 2007.

One thing is sure and true: in regard to the film *The Wonder Of It All*, William Rutledge knew what he was talking about, and he was also well-informed, apparently better than our Italian journalists (included myself in Europe). In consequence of this, I guess that for an insider as he claims to be, such a peculiar celebration could be known and an occasion of meeting and discussion.

And perhaps an excellent opportunity to carry out an intelligence operation for an unofficial disclosure of classified space missions.

CHAPTER XII

A Separate Space Program? Clues and a Comment by W. Cunningham On the Apollo 19 incident

The last century the USAF (the United States Air Force) developed its own Space program, to have manned missions. MOL-Gemini was of one of its projects.

MOL meant "Manned Orbiting Laboratory", a military Air Force space station, launched on board a Titan IIIC rocket into a polar orbit (that's why the Vandenberg Air Force Base – in California - was chosen as launching site, and in this particular case it was chosen the SLC-6, the so-called "Slick-6", as launching pad). But because of budget reasons (and also because of the growing success of the spy satellite program, not manned but automatic), in 1969 the Defense Secretary Melvin R. Laird decided to cancel the program (it became too expensive). Only one launch took place, in November 1966, but without crew.

We have to pay attention to the Space Launch Complex 6, at the Vandenberg Air Force Base, because it is mentioned by the insider with nickname of "moonwalker1966delta", the alleged Apollo 19 Commander, who would have been inside the Apollo spacecraft with its crew, on February the 2nd, 1976: at 05.30 AM Western time, the Saturn V rocket would have been launched to the Moon by secrecy (target: a landing on the far side to investigate some lunar anomalies, already discussed in the prevoius chapters).

In his comment on YouTube, the insider "moonwalker1966delta" says: <<*The only Apollo launch with a yellow tower and no NASA signs on the rocket as for Apollo 20*>>[37].

From the Kennedy Space Center in Florida it is possible to put spacecrafts (like the Apollo) into equatorial orbits, saving fuel thanks to the additional rotational speed of Earth at that latitude. From the

---

37 See the Appendix IV.

California coast it is easier launching into polar orbits. About the controversy if it is possible to put spacecrafts like the Apollo into space - even from Vandenberg - please read again the answer by "moonwalker1966delta", in my interview with him.

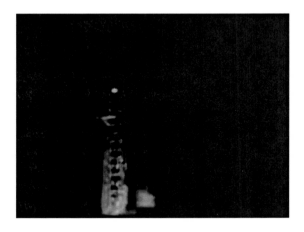

Frame (colors deleted) from the footage <<*APOLLO 19 LAUNCH*>> uploaded on YouTube by "moonwalker1966delta", on November 20, 2009.

The insider has commented on the launch tower was yellow (a very unusual color), and that the Saturn V rocket – which would have been launched from Vandenberg AFB, Complex 6, on February 2nd, 1976, at 05.30 Am Western time – had no NASA signs on it, as for Apollo 20.

Image credit: "moonwalker1966delta", YouTube;

reproduction by kind permission of "moonwalker1966delta"

Let us return now to the MOL program. In the third group of astronauts (all of them test pilots and from the military) for MOL-Gemini, there was also the first Afro-American chosen to fly from earth into outer Space: Robert H. Lawrence (Chicago, 1935 - 1967), who died because of an incident during a test flight (with an aircraft).

Therefore Lawrence – remembered as the Major Bob Lawrence by Walter Cunningham[38] (retired USMCR Colonel, and NASA astronaut

---

38 Dr. W. Cunningham (born on March 16, 1932, in Creston, Iowa) – a former scientist employed by Rand Corporation - was also the backup Lunar Module Pilot to the crew of Apollo 1. With Rand Corp. he worked on "classified defense studies and problems of the earth's magnetosphere", the Cunnigham's website says. At the end of his career at the Johnson Space Center, he was Chief of the Skylab Branch of the Fight Crew

with Apollo 7) in its essay *I ragazzi della Luna* (edited in Italy by Giovanni Caprara[39]) – would have been the first Afro-American to become an astronaut for the USA (but for the USAF, not NASA). Cunningham tells that the USAF officer and pilot died in a crash with its F-104.

William Rutledge (the Apollo 20 CDR) told me something more about the space history of African-Americans: it would have been Stephanie Ellis[40] one of the first Afro-Americans – thus after the death of Lawrence, we can conclude - to be chosen as astronaut (and – as Major Lawrence did – she also died before to fly in Space).

Of course, it is possible – if there are secret pages of space program as W. Rutledge claims – that not all the NASA astronauts are aware of that. Somebody could have the right "need to know". Others no.

An opinion of Walter Cunningham on the Apollo 19 incident: my question for him

At the end of September 2008 I wrote an e-mail to dr. Walter Cunningham, who is a former NASA astronaut and also a former Marine Corps fighter pilot. In the e-mail I asked him a comment about some statements made by the insider "moonwalker1966delta", but a comment "under the point of view of an astronaut". I asked him if the author of such statements could be a former astronaut, as "moonwalker1966delta" claims to be.

Here the statements I presented to him:

<<[...] *we still don't know what caused a light loss of gyroscopic inertial vector a sudden breakdown of electrical power bus unit and a completely loss of telemetry. We had smoke and light fire on the frontal panel but we have been able to extinguish it at once. As soon as we had electrical power*

Directorate.

39 Chapter XV, *Cambiano le selezioni*, pag.403, in the book *I ragazzi della Luna*, by Walter Cunningham, edited by Giovanni Caprara, Ugo Mursia Editore (Italian Publisher), translation by Umberto Cavallaro, Milano, 2009.

40 So, she would also have been – if they did not change the Apollo 19 crew - the first woman in Space for the US, not only the first Afro-American; but by secrecy; the Soviets already used crews with female members. Anyway, if Stephanie Ellis did exist indeed, she died at the end of 1975, according to the second insider ("moonwalker1966delta"), but not in Space as William Rutledge told me.

again we stopped manually giroscopic[41] *movement. Fortunatly*[42] *we still have radio contact with Houston and as soon as* [name omitted] *and* [name omitted] *entered the simulator we have been able to receive remote telemetry data in voice with* [name omitted] *and Houston.>>*

But in the e-mail I provided further information for him: I added an excerpt from a leak of information that took place before the publication of my interview with "moonwalker1966delta" (September 2008 and October 2008) . The revelation came from revver.com and its user "allojz1986".

"allojz1986" and his disclosure on Revver: the incident of Apollo 19 and much more

The revver user told the general public that – according to a "supposingly internal source" – Apollo 19 would have been launched on February 2nd, 1976[43]. The targets of the mission would have been to land South of Izsak D crater. About the EVAs (the extravehicular activities), EVA 1,2,3 were scheduled to visit the mothership[44], while the EVA 4 to investigate the City, and the EVA 5 and EVA 6 the base located Southeast of Delporte crater. He also commented the presence of triangular objects and the original Apollo 19 crew, with Stephanie Ellis and A. Sorokin.

So, I realized at the time that even "allojz1986" - this Revver user - knew the same information I had got (and others I had not) from my source "moonwalker1966delta"; then I thought that this presumed former NASA astronaut, had had several contacts and discussions with more than one person interested in the disclosure.

By the way, the precious leak of information by "allojz1986" convinced me to edit and spread my report-interview with

---

41 The right term is "gyroscopic", with the "y" letter instead of "girocscopic", with the "i". As the matter of fact, the above word is correct. So, just a mistake by the insider using the keyboard.

42 The right term should be "fortunately", instead of "fortunatly".

43 The date indicated here, is coherent with the date indicated later by "moonwalker1966delta", when he posted on YouTube the video of the presumed launch of Apollo 19, from the Vandenberg AFB, Complex 6 (YouTube, november 2009).

44 With the expression "mothership", he probably means the cigar-shaped object.

"moonwalker1966delta" as soon as possible. And I did it, at the end of September 2008 (first part of my interview). I think everybody interested in the case, should thank "allojz1986" for his precious contribution.

I do not know who "allojz1986" really is: on the revver.com I did not see any description on his profile, but on YouTube I found a user with the same nickname, interested on the same topic (the disclosure of "retiredafb") and so there is the chance that he is the same person: the YouTube profile I have found, it has a description of a young man from the Eastern Europe.

Anyway, either "allojz1986" on Revver has had contacts with "moonwalker1966delta", or he has had contacts with another source of information, perhaps in Europe: could it be that a former technician from USSR or a former Soviet astronaut involved in the ASTP, knows something about the classified missions of Apollo 19/20[45]? There is also a tiny possibility that even behind the nickname of "allojz1986" there could be a former astronaut from Eastern Europe or from the old USSR. Someone who knows the truth, or just fragments of hidden truth, as direct witness. Of course, in this last case he would not have told the truth about his identity. But for the moment I suppose he is just a young man indeed, as he says on his profile, in probable contact with "moonwalker1966delta".

"allojz1986" has spread on revver.com – as comment – the story of the incident of Apollo 19, a story already discussed by W. Rutledge ("retiredafb"): a few seconds before the engine stopped at the end of

---

45 For more information about the disclosure by "allojz1986", I invite the reader to search his comments on the discussion forum of revver.com. There are information about the Soviet cosmonaut <<*Aleksei Sorokin (reportedly deceased at January 11th 1976)*>> and about Stephanie Ellis, who <<*had to be part of the crew*>> (the first Apollo 19 crew). I knew already the name of Sorokin, because the first individual to mention the cosmonaut was "retiredafb", in a message sent to me in 2007, but that I did not disclose at the time, and only in the second interview with the Apollo 19 Commander. Among the disclosed information by "allojz1986" – on revver.com – there would be the real reasons behind the scenes of the decision of launching again manned missions to the Moon, and there are the lunar coordinates of the presumed triangular objects discussed by "moonwalker1966delta" in my interview: <<*[...] two triangular objects visible in AS15-P-9625 and AS15-P-9630 at the upper side of the pic and just right of the mothership at coordinates 18.7S -116.92E and 18.31S -117.48E.*>> So, this last information was disclosed by "allojz1986" in August 2008, and was coherent with the information already in my possession since July 2008 thanks to "moonwalker1966delta"; source: http://www.revver.com/u/retiredafb/

TLI maneuver of Apollo 20, there was a crash: the Apollo crew heard a "metallic bang". Probably something had hit the spacecraft in Space, causing fire on board, a loss of telemetry and <<*as much as unexpected amount of gyro angle position on Z*>>.

But fortunately, the Mission Control was still in contact with the crew, and the reentry – but without carrying out the mission in reaching the Moon with a landing - was possible through the difficult work made by the backup crew inside the simulator (on the ground) that tried to <<*synchronize movements and positions through the manual data sent from Apollo 19 crew*>>.

The comment by Walter Cunningham: "all pure nonsense", but no answer on the cigar-shaped object

In spite of the amount of technical details and concepts of space flight I gave him with my e-mail, the answer of dr. Walter Cunningham (Apollo 7) was very short:

<<*All pure nonsense. There never was an Apollo 19. All the dialogue is phoney. You can quote me.   Walt*>>[46]

Dr. W. Cunningham was very kind in sending me a quick answer. All the other former NASA astronauts I had asked - and who received my question - simply ignored it or they did not have time to answer. So, I thank dr. Cunningham for his kindness. He has proved to be a gentleman even with an unknown freelance writer like I was at the time.

So, now we can focus our attention on his comment: it is interesting to notice that his comment is "all pure nonsense" not because – it seems to me – the statements presented are not coherent with space flight and a possible situation of incident of an Apollo spacecraft in Space, but because "there never was an Apollo 19." Just a reason of official Space history.

But when in a following e-mail I asked him a comment about the cigar-shaped object resting on the far side of the Moon, I did not receive any answer. So, I said to myself: it is likely my further question was quite embarrassing for him. That's my opinion. We have also to remember that W. Cunningham was employed by NASA to investigate

---

46 E-mail by dr. Walter Cunningham sent to Luca Scantamburlo, September 22, 2008.

the reasons of the terrible incident of Apollo 1, occurred in 1967. His group of study was in charge to understand the safety measures. With him, his fellow astronauts Donn Eisele and Frank Borman. In his very interesting book of memoirs entitled *I ragazzi della Luna* (in its italian edition), Cunningham tells that his group of study listened the audio tapes of the incident, many times: they listened the dialogue between the astronauts, a few seconds before died[47]. So, dr. Cunningham is qualified, I guess, to have a serious opinion on such a presumed incident, taken place in Space, not on the ground: the Apollo 19 incident. Maybe, it is because of his former duty as member of a committee of inquiry for an incident (as consultant), that he has been sensible in answering me.

The Apollo 1 crew – as I have already explained before, in another chapter - died in a tragic accident on January 27, 1967, during a launch pad test of the Apollo/Saturn spacecraft being prepared for the first piloted flight: the AS-204 mission. Subsequently the AS-204 mission was re-designated Apollo 1 to remember the lost space crew. The NASA astronauts who died in that horrible way were: Edward Higgins White II (1930-1967), Virgil Ivan "Gus" Grissom (1926-1967), and Roger Chaffee (1935-1967).

Probably – as dr. Cunningham says in his book[48] – without their undesirable sacrifice, the Apollo program could have other problems, they could have not developed such a wonderful spacecraft as the Apollo became, and the Americans would have not reached the Moon only in 5 missions as they did, but much later.

---

47 See the chapter I, *"Abbiamo un incendio in cabina!"*, by Walter Cunningham, edited by Giovanni Caprara, Ugo Mursia Editore (Italian Publisher), translation by Umberto Cavallaro, Milan, 2009, pagg.33-36.

48 *I ragazzi della Luna*, ibidem, chapter I, page. 40 of the Italian edition. The North American reprojected and redeveloped the Apollo spacecraft, after the terrible incident taken place on the ground.

Clues on a separate Space program: Robert O. Dean speaks out

During the debate taken place in Barcelona at the end of July 2009 – at the *European Exopolitics Summit 2009. A New Paradigm for a World in Crisis* – Robert Orel Dean[49] (born in 1929, he is a retired U.S. Army Command Sergeant Major, Bob for his friends) told the public about a <<*separate space program*>> funded with the so-called black budget, and operative in the last decades.

In spite of he did not point any Apollo 19 and 20, the former U.S Army non-commissioned officer revealed something new: he had hesitated to speak out about it until then – he said - because of the <<*sensitivity of this subject*>>.

In Spain he told the audience that the U.S. have <<*a separate space program*>> and he mentioned not only the black budget for the DoD, but some launches in the last (over) 30 years from a variety of different places in USA; the U.S. Military have been launching from Vandenberg, from Area 51 in Nevada, from Utah, and from Pacific Islands (Kwajalein Atoll).

The Vandenberg Air Force Base in California – according to R. Dean –

---

49 Robert O. Dean – a U.S. Korea and Vietnam war veteran, highly decorated – has spent 27 years in the U.S. Army. He was also employed with the NATO as intelligence analyst in Europe, at the Supreme Headquarters Allied Powers in Europe (S.H.A.P.E.), from 1963 until 1967, with a "Cosmic Top Secret" security clearance, he claims. During an interview with the journalist Maurizio Baiata, for the Italian magazine *X Times* (nr. 6, April 2009) Bob Dean showed his military credentials, published on that issue. From 1963 until 1970 he had secret duties, whose access was reserved to whom in possession of a "need to know". Many medals are testimony of his duty for the U.S. Army: the Korean Service Medal (1 campaign), the United Nations Service Medal and the Vietnam Service Medal; I remember particularly his Bronze Star Medal and Purple Heart (1st OLC). His son is a retired U.S. NAVY officer, who worked at the Pentagon. Dean has been carrying out his unofficial disclosure program since 1993. One of his most important remarks was published on *The New York Times*, on November 21, 1993. The title of the article was <<*For U.F.O. Fans, Question Is Not 'If?' but 'How Was the Trip?'*>>, by Douglas Martin. The article discussed the meeting organized at the Ramada Pennsylvania Hotel, at Seventh Avenue and 33d Street, where many experts spoke out about the UFO phenomenon and its cover-up by world's Governments, especially Washington. Robert Dean told the news conference that he had gathered a group of Generals and Admirals, as well as astronauts and cosmonauts, well prepared to testify before the public and crumble the cover-up. This group of ranking officers – but the article did no say - is the so-called "Old Boys Network". In many occasions, later on in the following years, Dean mentioned it and included as members of this Network even some Jesuits (consult the article <<*Bob Dean is flying high*>>, published on *TucsonWeekly*, by Jim Nintzel and Héctor Acuña, Volume 12, Number 16 . June 29 - July 5, 1995).

is one the space sites used for launching spacecrafts of this separate space program. Did he mean launching manned spacecrafts? The Vandenberg AFB is just the AFB mentioned by W. Rutledge and "moonwalker1966delta", as launch site for Apollo 19 and 20.

But the Vandenberg AFB is famous also because of a famous article written in the late 1980s by a well-known journalist and writer: William J. Broad.

The New York Times, 1989: the article by William J. Broad about the the DoD clandestine program of military astronauts

The New York Times published on August 7, 1989, an article by W. J. Broad entitled <<Pentagon Leaves the Shuttle Program>>[50]. In the article there was the story of a group of military astronauts (32) located in Los Angeles, and trained for flying the Space Shuttle fleet for the DoD (USAF). Broad is an accomplished journalist as science correspondent, author or co-author of many essays. Moreover, during his career Broad has won two Pulitzer Prizes with his NYT fellow journalists, so we can rely on his reports.

In the years 1984-85 there were – according to Broad and his source of information – more than 4000 people involved in such a military program. The Vandenberg AFB was chosen as site from where to launch the Space Shuttles for the DoD, but the Space Shuttle Challenger incident that occurred in January 1986 was the main reason why the Pentagon decided to end the program.

Billions of dollars spent since the end of the 1970s, and a spaceport (Vandenberg) apparently never used for military crews. The DoD project was a joint military and civilian program (NASA took part in it). The name of the military astronauts groups in Los Angeles for this "clandestine program" – according to W. J. Broad – was "Manned Spaceflight Engineer Program", founded by the Air Force Space Division (Division of USAF).

So, the main target for the Pentagon was to take advantage of the NASA achievements to launch top-secret payloads, and that's why they began to develop another Mission Shuttle Control, only for classified missions, located in Colorado at the edge of the Rocky Mountains. I

---

50 <<Pentagon Leave the Shuttle Program>>, by William J. Broad, The New York Times, August 7, 1989, page A13 of the New York edition.

invite the reader to obtain the original article by Broad for further details.

The David Scott's testimony: the U.S. Air Force top-secret "Blue shuttle" program

Another confirmation of this classified space program, comes from an autobiography by David Scott[51] (written, by the way, with Alexei Leonov): in his pages the former NASA astronaut D. Scott describes his involvement in a <<*top-secret program training Air Force officers*>>. It is the same program described by W. J. Broad: the name is just "Manned Spaceflight Engineer" (same expression used by the *NYT* science correspondent) or MSE project, Scott says.

The former Apollo astronaut D. Scott was approached by the USAF to take part in that program. With him, some of the best engineers employed with the Apollo program. The USAF – as Broad told on *The New York Times* pages – was going to develop its own new space program, with – Scott says – its "blue shuttles", that the Air Force was planning to project and build. In Los Angeles – Scott tells his readers – there was the training of MSEs astronauts, and he was in charge with others to select and assist the training of the first two groups of new USAF astronauts, later on employed in regular NASA flights (not blue shuttles yet). But everything – as we already know – was cancelled.

If such a secret Shuttle space program was possible and remained a hush-hush project until the publication of the Broad's article (1989), why there might not be other Pentagon secrets concerning Apollo classified missions in the late 1970s, to send to the far side of the Moon a joint US and USSR crew, after the well-known ASTP[52]?

And why David Scott was approached and chosen for training and assisting the new USAF astronauts? Is it possible that USAF trusted him because of a previous his involvement in another classified space program, taken place in the 1970s? It is just my working hypothesis, not a rumor. I will discuss it in the following chapter (XIII).

---

51 *Two Sides of the Moon. Our Story of the Cold War Space Race*, by David Scott and Alexei Leonov, with Christine Toomey, Thomas Dunne Books, St. Martin's Press, New York, October 2004, pages 381-382.

52 Apollo Soyuz Test Project (July 1975), a joint US and USSR space program (Apollo 18 according to a NASA information on-line, already discussed by me, and the Soyuz 19).

Clues from the past: Dr. Peter Beter and Milton William Cooper

If we have a look at the testimonies of the past, we find something of interesting in the famous *Casebook on Alternative 3: UFOs, Secret Societies and World Control*, a wonderful book written by Kim Keith (editor of the *Gemstone File*, IllumiNet Press, 1992). In his essay, at the chapter 16 – <<*Lunar Base Alpha One*>> – there is a reference to what happened in 1973 at Diego Garcia, the same island of the Indian Ocean indicated by John Lear in his e-mail sent to me in the year 2007 (see the footnote of the chapter VIII, <<*An Interview With Apollo 19 Commander*>>).

John Lear is the retired American pilot I mention in my interview with the Apollo 19 Commander, but whose name I have kept secret until the publication of this book. Jim Keith points out in his book[53] – on the basis of dr. Peter Beter statements – that <<*a secret American space program*>> did exist at the time, and the fact that launching Eastwards from the Diego Garcia Island was a suitable choice, because the great amount of water of open sea which surrounds the island.

Milton William Cooper (1943-2001) – a controversial radio host and former petty officer who was killed at home (just outside his house) in Eagar (Arizona) on November 6, 2001 – made in the past some remarkable statements about the presence on the Moon of "motherships". Did he get any classified information of what became the target for the Apollo 19 and 20 missions?

In his *Operation Majority* - a text he spread on Internet at the end of 1980s – M.W. "Bill" Cooper discussed a presumed alien base on the far side of the Moon, filmed by Apollo astronauts, and wrote something concerning: << [...] *the very large alien craft which have been described in various sighting reports as "MOTHER SHIPS" are based there*>>.[54]

---

53 *Casebook on Alternative 3: UFOs, Secret Societies and World Control*, by Jim Keith, chapter 16 "Lunar Base Alpha One", IllumiNet Press, Lilburn, GA, USA, 1994, pages 110-111.

54 *OPERATION MAJORITY*, by Milton William Cooper, 1989. Cooper was a former U.S. Air Force, and later a Navy petty officer. He was also a Vietnam war veteran, and an author of many books about conspiracy theories, UFOs, shadow governments. Cooper went on a lecture tour several times in U.S., talking of the presence of an extraterrestrial intelligence on our planet (especially in its oceans). For more information on Cooper's life: *The Hour of Our Time, The Legacy of William Cooper* is a good video documentary – dedicated to him - to begin. If someone is interested in books, his most famous work is *Behold a Pale Horse*. M. W. Cooper served on the Intelligence briefing team of the ONI (Office of Naval Intelligence), in the Pacific Fleet. Cooper was killed in November 2001 by the Apache County Sheriff Department, during a shooting.

In my opinion it is an indirect confirmation of the story told us by William Rutledge (the Apollo 20 Commander): it is true that Apollo 15 and 17 crews took pictures of a cigar-shaped object on the dark side of the Moon; an object which seems just a very large alien craft, pointed by Rutledge as an ancient alien mothership.

So, we have another circumstantial evidence (by Milton William Cooper) apparently connected to the Apollo 19 and 20 disclosure, enough far-off from the Rutledge's testimony.

CHAPTER XIII

Apollo 19 and 20:
My Further Revelations

Why did I rely on these insiders? It is a legitimate question. Of course, their testimony is controversial, because of many aspects of contradiction and because of some video fakes (above all from "retiredafb"'s material). But I have found too many coincidences and small details of history which seem to fit into each other, in a judicious context. Let us begin from the presumed presence of Alexei Leonov in San Antonio (Texas) in the early 1990s.

Clues on a meeting between David Scott and Alexei Leonov, in 1993: yes, it is true, at least in NYC

In my interview with "moonwalker1966delta", the alleged Apollo 19 Commander and former NASA astronaut has claimed he met A. Leonov – with William Rutledge, David Scott (Apollo 15) and L.M. Snyder – in a restaurant in San Antonio, in 1993 (chapter VIII, answers to my questions nr. 4 and 5, first part of the interview). Keep in mind this year, please: 1993.

Is there any record of this visit? I have been doing a long research, and some months ago I found a small key evidence: in the essay *Two Sides of the Moon. Our Story of Cold War Space Race*, by David Scott and Alexei Leonov; at the end of the book there is written that Leonov was in New York City with David Scott, at dinner, "twenty years later"[55] the historical visit - occurred in 1973 in USSR - of the U.S. delegation led by David Scott. The American delegation had to negotiate with the Soviets all the technical aspects of the important joint US/USSR space mission: the Apollo Soyuz Test Project (ASTP). This means that Leonov was in USA in 1993 (1973 plus 20 is 1993), at least on the East coast (New York City). It is likely that he went somewhere else, during his stay in the

---

55 *Acknowledgments*, by David Scott, page 391, from the essay *Two Sides of the Moon. Our Story of the Cold War Space Race*, by David Scott and Alexei Leonov, with Christine Toomey, Thomas Dunne Books, St. Martin's Press, New York, October 2004.

135

United States. Did he go to San Antonio (Texas), as "moonwakler1966delta" claims? We do not know, so far. But Leonov met Scott in 1993, and this is an important key evidence.

David Scott himself recollects his meeting and dinner with Leonov in NYC, in 1993. And San Antonio – one of the biggest American cities, with a strong military presence and many important historical and cultural scenes - is a place important for some NASA astronauts' life, especially for Leonov himself.

Moreover, David Scott, was born in San Antonio (on June 6, 1932, at Randolph Air Force Base), and this could explain why Scott would have been in San Antonio in 1993 (his place of birth). But for sure the Soviet cosmonaut was in San Antonio in the 1970s, at the Folklife Festival: NASA itself says that, and there is a picture of Leonov – while he is dancing with a belly dancer – taken on September 14, 1974 (site of San Antonio's HemisFair).[56]

Of course the presence of Leonov at the time was due to his involvement with the Apollo Soyuz Test Project, as one of two members of the prime Soviet crew. Leonov was trained at the Johnson Space Center, in Houston (there are pictures of him, taken for example in April 1974, where we can see Alexei Leonov at the Building 35 of JSC; in one picture, he is even handling a Westinghouse TV camera).

We know also that Leonov probably came back to San Antonio in 2006. On Internet I have found an important evidence of that: in August 2006 there was a meeting with Space pioneers, and there was Leonov, according to the testimony of a collector and fond of space.[57] So the city of San Antonio – it seems to me – is a place full of memories for the former General and cosmonaut, visited by him more than one time. Moreover, in San Antonio – at Brooks AFB - there were some "exhaustive medical texts" to select the first astronauts. You can find the reference in the Cernan's book: *The Last Man on the Moon*, written with Don Davis.[58]

---

56 http://science.ksc.nasa.gov/mirrors/images/images/pao/ASTP/10076465.htm
Cosmonaut Aleksey Leonov joins belly dancer on stage at Folklife Festival. NASA Photo ID: S74-28666

57 Read the interesting article by Larry McGlyn: <<*Alexei Leonov: A Soul in Space*>> posted on Friday, September 05, 2008.

http://spacearttribute.blogspot.com/2006/03/cosmonauts-as-artists.html

58 Pag.58, *Max and Deke*, chapter VII, *The Last Man on the Moon*, by Cernan and Davis,

Year 2007: the William Rutledge's invitation to a "special friend who is well known in space community"

Now my first revelation: I did not pay too much attention to a small detail, as I have already told you at the end of the chapter IX: on June 6, 2007, in a YouTube message sent to me, William Rutledge wrote he was going to invite a <<*special friend who is well known in space community*>>.

I did not recall and think about this detail until the beginning of January 2010, when I had the chance to review all my files, documents and papers.

Not, it seems to me that this special friend – if "retiredafb" and "moonwalker196delta" are insiders indeed, and not the same person or two hoaxers – could be just the YouTube user "moonwalker1966delta", maybe convinced by William Rutledge to come forward.

Other clues on William Rutledge's knowledge of space flight and Apollo procedures, are contained in that message. The discussion is about the contamination of Apollo 20 footage with Apollo 11 footage: audio (which contaminates the presumed lift-off of Apollo 20) and video (frames which pollute the beginning of the presumed LM-15 flyover video, on the Moon). Here you are an excerpt of that, without any correction by me, as usual (part of it already disclosed, and part of it unpublished until the publication of this book):

> <<[...] *One day, i'll invite a special friend who is well known in space community, it could be a good surprise.*
>
> *Abut the soundtrack, i think you'r right, ididn't compare the sound, but some tapes are polluted with apollo 11 , sometimes it is a question of one or two frames. A youtube poster showed me frames from the flyover video, i didn't notice that.*
>
> *One bravo was an abort procedure, we had ONE A B ONE C which allowed us to control thrusters on the LES (escape tower). IMHO, only apollo 12 was effectively using ONE bravo, after being hit by a lightning strike, but Alan Bean commuted from SCE to AUX to override and continue the flight.*
>
> *Anyway, i have no apollo 11 tapes, i can't compare it about soundtrack, but i'll be more carefull about the title pages. I'll rip off some sound or title pages if necessary.*

Chapter 7, St. Martin's Griffin, New York, USA, 1999, Tenth Anniversary Edition, June 2009.

Honestly, the material has nothing common with apollo 11. On the lift off sequence, the saturn 5 has no markings till the third stage. the S IV b had "CCCP" and "USAF" markings, it was the only part marked, because S IV b never get back to earth, the other stages had to fall into the sea and could'nt were markings. µBecause of this lack of markings, one youtuber told the community he recognize a saturn 1b, which could not be powerfull enough to send LM+CSM to the moon. In vandenberg, the saturn V launch had to be not reconizable, no BW lines or USA marks on the rocket. Only the last ring was black painted, and it could look like an ordinary DElta rocket at 4 miles distance. I know it can be confusing for peoples, [...]>>

June 06, 2007, 01:37 AM, from a "retiredafb's message" to Luca Scantamburlo's YouTube account

I have always had the impression that – at least part of it (maybe the beginning) - the footage named <<*APOLLO 20 launch feed stage 1 and interstaging unit separation*>> uploaded in January 2008 by "retiredafb" on revver.com, is a computer graphic work, perhaps based on an original Apollo footage (so we could have an editing of a fake and an authentic footage); does it make any sense comparing the film with what Rutledge wrote? No markings until the third stage, he said: but on the presumed first stage we can see what it looks like a marking.

Anyway, the altitude of the rocket - when the separation of the first stage takes place - is enough coherent with what "moonwalker1966delta" said in my interview with him.[59] Much higher than previous Apollo missions, and for good reasons as he explains.

Another thing to point: some Revver.com and YouTube users – very attentive – has recognized in that footage a landscape which does not look like the American coast, but an African Coast and the Middle East, we can say. They have written their comments on the Web. Could it be in accordance with a possible launch from Diego Garcia Island? I do not know. If these presumed missions did take place indeed, it is possible that after a launch from Vandenberg, in February 1976 (Apollo 19), the following mission (Apollo 20, taken place in August 1976) has been launched from the Diego Garcia Island - as suggested by John Lear – but, I suppose, maintaining Vandenberg as Mission Control Center.

---

59 <<*But if you take a look at the first stage separation footage of Apollo 11 for example and the Apollo 20 Rutldedge's footage you will notice for sure that the altitude it separated at is much much higher then apollo 11 altitude and the separation speed is much slower and the only reason for it is to make the first and second stage to be yet attracted by earth gravity but enough high to ensure they completely destroy during reentry into the atmosphere.*>>, from the answer to question nr. 1, Chapter VIII.

That' s just my opinion. I could be wrong. But what we can watch in the footage – the presumed first stage (S-IC) after the separation from the point of view of a probable camera fixed on the interstage – is not the Saturn V third stage (S-IVB), that was used twice during the launch of an Apollo mission and had a single engine (not 5 engines like the first stage) with restart capability: the first ignition of S-IVB was necessary to inject the Apollo spacecraft into earth orbit; the second ignition was used to set the spacecraft into a translunar trajectory from Earth orbit. According to "retiredafb" only the Saturn V stage S-IVB had markings. So, I do not understand the comment by "retiredafb" on revver.com, when he says: <<*Separation of stage one an interstage unit, the USAF and CCCP markings are slightly visible on some pictures.*>> What does it mean? That on the other stages there were writings, but very small compared to the usual markings of a Saturn V ("USA" marking, for example)?

If we had been able to see in the footage the separation of the third stage (SIV-B), that could be the stage marked with the CCCP acronym, and with the last ring black painted, as William Rutledge told me and claimed. This is not the case. But my knowledge of space flight and space history is not great (I am too young and I am not a specialist), so it is difficult for me to say what the footage represents. But I agree with the opinion expressed by "allojz1986", Revver and YouTube user. The reader should remember who he is: again, he helpes the discussion with comments posted on Web, but on Revver.com in this occasion: he explains that the first part of the footage is filmed by the first camera on Saturn V S-II (the second stage), while most of the footage (so it is an editing) shows from the point of view of the second camera, fixed inside the interstage module, floating in Space.

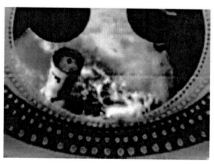

Frame B/W (colours deleted) from the video <<*APOLLO 20 launch feed stage 1 and interstaging unit separation*>>, uploaded in January 2008 by "retiredafb" on revver.com
Image credit: "retiredafb", Revver;

The CCCP marking on the SIVB? The Apollo 19 incident and its footage details

Before I disclosed this Rutledge's information about possible CCCP and USAF markings only on the last stage of the rocket,[60] I had received - in December 2009 – an e-mail from a source of mine (we call him "a Chinese"), in which he attached an analysis of the footage, and telling me what he believed to be the marking of "CCCP" visible on the rocket stage, floating free in Space (snapshot at time: 03'57"). The CCCP is – of course – the well-known acronym used for the USSR. This, in my opinion, would be a strange contradiction if confirmed, which would give less credibility to the William Rutledge's testimony. It seems there is a marking close to the what looks like a black ring on the upper part, but I cannot read it. On the contrary, it is true that the presumed lift-off from Vandenberg AFB, uploaded on YouTube in 2007, showed a very unusual rocket as colours and painting, very different from a normal Saturn V. And this is in accordance with the Rutledge's testimony. A part from the audio, which comes from an Apollo previous mission.

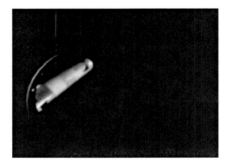

Frame B/W (colours deleted) from the video <<*APOLLO 20 launch feed stage 1 and interstaging unit separation*>>, uploaded in 2008 by "retiredafb" on revver.com Presumed Saturn V first stage, after its separation. Notice what looks like a marking, just below a sort of black ring.

Image credit: "retiredafb", Revver;

reproduction by kind permission of "retiredafb" (William Rutledge)

---

60 The Saturn V rocket had three stages: the first was the S-IC (usually used for 2'30", to reach an altitude of 66 km), the second the S-II (usually used for 5'59", to reach an altitude of 185 km), and the third one was the S-IVB (used twice, for 8'); is the one mentioned by William Rutledge as the only stage with markings for the Apollo 20 mission, according to him? About the dimensions of the last stage, we have as height of 17.8 meters, and a diameter of 6.6 meters.

However the same anonymous source – this Chinese individual – showed me his personal work of image comparison among the frames from the Apollo 19 incident YouTube video (a 16 mm footage), and the interior of the Apollo spacecraft.

It seems that the details visible in the footage uploaded by "moonwalker1966delta", are the same details that it is possible to recognize watching carefully the panel instruments of an Apollo spacecraft. Of course, if the Apollo 19 incident footage is an authentic film, it is possible that the crew is not visible because busy on the frontal panel of the spacecraft (in fact, the footage itself shows what it looks like the lateral part of the spacecraft instruments).

The meaning of DPI? The "moonwalker1966delta" answers

In December 2009 I asked "moonwalker1966delta" (the Apollo 19 Commander) what DPI means in the context of the footage *<<Apollo 20 preparing for DPI>>*, uploaded on YouTube by him on February 12, 2008 (see the Appendix IV), and which as introduction has a DoD marking and a warning ("internal use copy" and "not for general..."). The footage seems an editing. In its second part is clearly visible the lunar surface, through the LEM window. The LEM seems in lunar orbit yet.

The insider ("moonwalker1966delta") gave me a technical explanation (a little too much for a simple hoaxer, as many individuals claim) that I reproduce as follows:

> *<<DPI or PDI is nothing then the acronym for Powered Descent Initiation that is the second phase of braking phases on lunar orbit right to the motion surface.*
>
> *The first is called DOI (Descent Orbit insertion) that is a retrograde manouver that is made in the orbit 180° and called Hohmann type transfer. It is made to reduce the altitude from about 60/70 nautical miles to 50000 feet. At this point DPI initiates and it's devided in 3 phases. The breaking phase to reduce orbit velocity, the approach phase that is controlled visually by pilot and the landing phase made to override automatic guidance for final approach and landing.>>*

December 05, 2009, from a moonwalker1966delta's message to Luca Scantamburlo's YouTube account

Frame (colors deleted) from the footage *<<Apollo 20 preparing for DPI>>* uploaded on YouTube by "moonwalker1966delta", on February 12, 2008.

Image credit: "moonwalker1966delta", YouTube;

reproduction by kind permission of "moonwalker1966delta"

What I have had not disclosed yet: the William Rutledge's revelations on alien technology

I reproduce here – for the first time – most of what William Rutledge wrote in his messages, dated May 23, 2007 (06:12 AM), before my written interview with him took place. I guess it is the right moment to do it. Not because of my book (many of his information have been already spread by me and published, for the general public, on Internet and on magazines, and someone could recognize some of them, reproduced again here), but because in the context of this astonishing disclosure, I believe it will be easier for the reader to understand me, above all after the reading of many pages of investigation.

It will be easier for you to understand my feelings of those days, back to the end of May 2007, and my shock. As usual, I do not correct his text (mistakes and wrong English form are his stamp):

<<[...] about nation involved:

1 As far as i know, it's USA and Russia, but i would not be surprised if france is on this program, MHD and anti matter is used in this country.

technology on triangle ships

2 Yes, many technology were found, corso spoke about some of them, but i'm surprised he didn't tell more. In the 0947 six ships, you know about fiber optics, mylar , integrated chips. But other were found:

a kinf of transparent steel, this was a micro perforated metal used in pressure disks, used apparently to establish soft equalization pf pressure, and it had a transparent property.

Metal with memory of form. After the accident, next morning, some parts of the craft were regaing the original shape.

Cloth computer, that is the only name i can find, there was a computer printed on a large piece of cloth, fibers were made with differents kind of metal connected, it was metal fibers with gradient of property. The memory blocks were lines of fiber silicon with prium. The internal clock was made with polonium. It seems to the engineers that the computer was not analogic, not binary, but had symbolic processors. This mean instead of comparing, "this is equal to that", the answer could be "this is the symbol of that", that is the founding of artifical intelligence. What was amazin was to deploy this piece of computer, and on maicroscope, it's a marvel to see silver, gold, silicon, other materials connected together.

About propulsion, the wing border is covered with electrods, spaced by 10 cm, who receive 300volts, the total power of the ship is 30teslas. The MHD main propulsion is helped by othe mhd brakes, a ionized layer is produced on the surface of the ship from a honeycomb barniment, which protect the ship at high speeds. The friction against molecules at high speed is used by the mhd motor to re aliment the main motor.

But the main information on trangular ships was, the massive amount of gold used inside.

apollo 19

3 Apollo 19 had a loss of telemetry wheile being at the end of the TLI, it was not clearly explained at this time, but it is beleived, it was a natural phenomemon, a collision of the aircraft and one of Cruithne brother, who was not identified in 1976.

since 1976

4 No return to the moon, and some unverified informations i have tell me that the spaceship was destructed november 7 2003, 1 achance on two it was not a natural>>

Computer Clothes?

About possible "computer clothes" mentioned by William Rutledge in his message dated May 2007, now the reader should remember the footage <<APOLLO 20 E.B.E. MonaLisa 16 mm film>>, uploaded by "retiredafb" on revver.com, on April 7, 2008; in the footage which we can see what look like findings/evidence of these so-called "computer clothes".

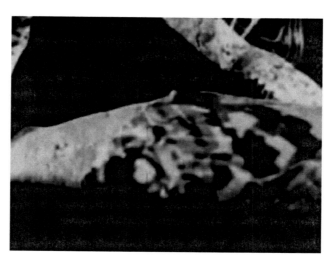

144

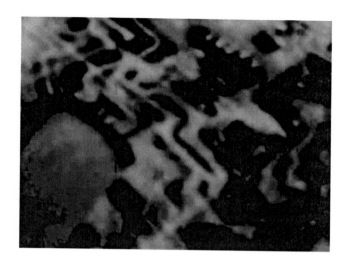

Frames B/W (colours deleted) from the video <<*APOLLO 20 E.B.E. MonaLisa 16 mm film*>>, uploaded on April 7, 2008, by "retiredafb" on revver.com ; are they possible evidence of the so-called "computer clothes", as William Rutledge called them?

Image credit: "retiredafb", Revver;

reproduction by kind permission of "retiredafb" (William Rutledge)

But let us have a look to another message by William Rutledge, sent to me in the same day (May 23, 2007, 07:22 AM):

<<[...] il'll post other pics, video from the russian probe, stable 16 mm film from CSM flyover, good colors, sharp image.

(landscape comparison as15-sills from videos)

About landsape, they are different, thats true, as15 9625 has ceen made 5 years sooner, and with different sun position, relief of the moon change very much with the light, and as15 is a low quality picture, we had an elliptical orbit 70km-120 km which allowed better pics. See the video of the other nasa pics of the ship, there are even more differences, the landscape is not reognizable, only the ship is a good reference.

EBE living? Honestly i prefer not answer now, i just would like to send the video of a EBE unconscious.

We know more about the homeworld of EBE using the triangles, we know that thay don't have the same meteorology than earth, the clpud coverage is *low, sun is rarely visible, there is a continuous discharge of energy in clouds, they dont know wghat thunder or lightning strike is, that's why the alamogordo (or socalled roswell) accident occured.>>*

From a following message (same date, May 23, 2007, 07:42 AM):

<<[...] about the spacecraft, one triangle was accessible)

in a triangle craft, we found two bodies, one in bad condition, a meteor cut the body at the neck level, we tok the littl skull on board.

The other body was strange, NDNA, not dead not alive, but crusted with impacts, stalagmites of blood coming out of hemmoragias zones. One body was on apollo 20, fixed on a hammock, and we passed hours watching the hands, the strange hair, not the kind you see a scifi movie. The hair was in good condition, we can say alive, alexei tested it.

The ship was not explored on the 4 kilometers, but no place detected for weapons.>>

And another one by "retiredafb", from the same date (May 23, 2007,07:48 AM), and with the usual mistakes, but also with an outstanding revelation about reverse engineering on alien technology, which would have helped the Americans to build the Memory block for the AGC (Apollo Guidance Computer):

<<[...] six craft fel on earth between alamogordo and roswell, 5 in alamogordo. All were hit by lightning streks, on had problems ans crashed later. The analyse showed that these aircrafts used ionized palsma around the "plane", with a power of 30 teslas, diffused by electrods on the wings, producing 300 volts on the top of the wings. It had be deducted that these ships come a world where thunder and strikes do not occur, energy discharge is continuous, and it's not a surprise they fell after a lightning strike hit.

I have a movie depicting the trensfer of transistor to integratd circuits for building Memory block for the apollo AGC computer.

Verification was, classifying a craft as e weapon, trnsportation craft, exploring ship, affecting an age to the vraft, and see if bodies you be the seme kind of those found on earth. The response was

-no military craft, exploring one, Crew of 300, two female pilot on trangles. Age is at least 15 miliardss of years. A colection of artifacts wering calligraphy, all made of gold, and computer clothes, the supreme state of computer , using fibers to overpass the traditionnal wiring, chips.>>

Frame B/W (colours deleted) from the video <<*APOLLO 20 E.B.E. MonaLisa 16 mm*>>, uploaded on April 7, 2008, by "retiredafb" on revver.com; are they possible findings/evidence of the collection of artifacts brought back to earth from the Moon, and made of gold?

Image credit: "retiredafb", Revver;

reproduction by kind permission of "retiredafb" (William Rutledge)

The new backup crew for Apollo 19: Neil Armstrong and Buzz Aldrin?

I have decided to reveal what "moonwalker1966delta" told me on May 12, 2008, about the backup crew that would have helped the prime crew of Apollo 19, in February 1976, in the difficult situation occurred in space, at the end of TLI. I mean the astronauts names who would have worked at the KSC, inside the simulator, and helped on radio – through Houston Mission Control - the prime crew in Space: the Apollo 19 crew. I have reasons to believe the testimony granted by "moonwalker1966delta". The main reason is because – after my long inquiry as journalist and freelancer - I have finally found a very interesting statement made by Neil Armstrong (Gemini 8, Apollo 11) in 1994, at the White House I guess, during the 25th Anniversary of the US landing on the Moon (Apollo 11, July 1969). It is a very cryptic statement – discussed by many in US, especially by Richard Hoagland – and says (the transcription is mine):

> <<[...] To you we say: we have only completed the beginning. We leave you much that is undone. There are great ideas undiscovered. Breakthroughs available to those who can remove one of truth's protective layers...>>[61]

Neil Armstrong

USA, 1994

Armstrong was in front of some American students, and he addressed the speech to them, to inspire young generations with hope. What did he mean about "one of truth's protective layers"?

It is my opinion that Neil Armstrong – like some other NASA astronauts - is aware of signs of extraterrestrial presence in the Solar System, and there is the possibility he was really involved as astronaut in classified military programs, to investigate some lunar anomalies. Of course, to speak out he would need an immunity from prosecution for violating his secrecy oaths.

I could be wrong, of course, but I have provided many details to the reader. Judge by yourself the "moonwalker1966delta" disclosure in his message (I have omitted some parts):

---

61 The Armstrong speech is available as video at the NBC News Archive.

[...] yes, I am a former astronaut. I have been Apollo CMDR and since William decided to tell the truth I think it's the right moment to do the same. I really don't know nor understand why William we had been lost in space. That's not true. It's true we have been hit by something few second before ending TLI manouver but thanks Neil and Buzz (our back up crew) we are still here to tell our story [...] fortunatly we still have radio contact with Houston and as soon as Neil and Buzz entered the simulator we have been able to receive remote telemetry data in voice with Neil and Houston. We had to be back up crew of Apollo 19 but since the original crew has been cancelled 3 weeks before launch we became the mission crew while Neil Armstrong and Buzz Aldrin have been selected as back up crew. [...] we haven't got women an board but another official Apollo program astronaut as pilot and another russian cosmonaut with exceptional medical skills. [...]>>

May 12, 2008, from a moonwalker1966delta's message to Luca Scantamburlo's YouTube account

The new revelations coming from YouTube discussions

Some very clever and patient YouTube users[62] were able to have public contact with "moonwalker1966delta". Questions and answers have been taking place on YouTube, and this helps to have a better comprehension and more information on the case, directly from the main insider on stage now: the alleged Apollo 19 Commander.

From these discussions we know – according to "moonwalker1966delta" - that:

1) the Apollo 19 astronauts were picked up in the Ocean by USS John F. Kennedy, while the Apollo 20 crew was picked up by USS Enterprise;

2) A. Sorokin was probably replaced by Yuri Romanenko[63], who

---

62 YouTube users "zikjames", "mikevlove" and "colkilgore".

63 Yuri Viktorovich Romanenko (1944, USSR), retired Colonel of Soviet and Russian Air Forces and former cosmonaut, highly decorated (as Hero of Soviet Union, for example). His last space flight as cosmonaut took place in 1987, with a Soyuz. For an interesting biography, consult http://www.spacefacts.de/english/bio_cosm.htm *Biographies of USSR/ Russian Cosmonauts.* In some biographical notes (Wikipedia), I have found one of his parents was a combat medic, and this could explain why "moonwalker1966delta" said the new Russian cosmonaut chosen for Apollo 19, had "exceptional medical skills". He could be Y. V. Romanenko.

became the Russian cosmonaut on aboard the Apollo 19, for the Soviets (but neither confirmed nor denied by "moonwalker1966delta" so far, who has just answered to the YouTube user "mikevlove" that Stephanie Ellis and Alexei Sorokin (original crew members for Apollo 19) <<*have been simply dismissed by the program and the back up crew took their place about 3 weeks before the launch date*>>;

3) About the Apollo 19 incident and how the astronauts resolved the problem, "moonwalker1966delta" said that unfortunately <<<*it is very hard to answer here explaining how the Apollo gyrostabilized platform works because the limited characters allowed anyway we used our AGS to stabylize the inertial movement caused by the impact and helped by back up crew using the simulator at KSC*>>

The idea that an Apollo backup crew were always ready to fly into Space, could seem not realistic, but what "moonwalker1966delta" says is in accordance with what the situation was at the time, at NASA. For example, in his memoirs *I ragazzi della Luna* (in its Italian edition), Walter Cunningham (Apollo 7) says - at the beginning of the chapter VII[64] - that theoretically the backup crews had always to be ready, to replace the prime crews. Another small detail of history of Apollo space program, known by the second deep throat.

Information by William Rutledge from *Cyberspaceorbit*

Years ago at the following link (of the website *Cyberspaceorbit.com*) was published, what I believe to be a discussion among William Rutledge and some Internet users, taken place in 2007:

http://www.cyberspaceorbit.com/retiredafb.html

I have asked the permission to reproduce some passages, to the responsible of the Website; he gave me his kind consent, above all, I suppose, in memory of Kent Moedl Steadman (1942 – 2008), who managed the website at the time, before him, and was one of the first

---

64   Pag. 161, Chapter VII, <<*Conteggio alla rovescia per l'Apollo 7*>>, essay *I ragazzi della luna*, by Walter Cunningham, edited by Giovanni Caprara, Ugo Mursia Editore, Italian edition, Milan (Italy), 2009, translation by Umberto Cavallaro.

persons to understand the importance of the disclosure by William Rutledge ("retiredafb"), and one of the first to link the topic to my website and my English articles, published since May 2007.

Kent was a highly respected art teacher, for many years, and a pioneer on the World Wide Web, with his site, http://www.cyberspaceorbit.com/[65]. I thank him in these pages, honoring his contribution for the Apollo 20 disclosure. I do not know if the discussion was reproduced by Kent himself because it was born through his *Cyberspaceorbit*, or it had taken place not on his forum but somewhere else on Web. It could come from comments of a files sharing community, comments that have been cancelled. Anyway, for this reason, I copy here only the William Rutledge's text (his answers to comments):

About the strange presence of frames from Apollo 11 footage, and included as introduction of one of the videos uploaded by "retiredafb" (the flyover, before the descent of the LEM), the question by "retiredafb" to the Web public is the following:

> <<*Please tell me which seconds you see "apollo 11" on this film? Craters shown are recognizable. The dsky shows Verb 15 noun 05 prog 34. Interferences, marks on the lem window are not subject of any comment, it would be strange not to find them [...]>>*

After the observation made by the Internet user, who points out where in the video there is the contamination, "retiredafb" answers:

> <<*you'r right, wrong title, should not be this one, but compare the video to apollo 11 or other missions, you won't ever ever find this moon flyover , craters lutke and delporte, compare the coordinates given on a lunar map . Only apollo 15 and 17 passed right over these craters before, and this film is not one of these mission. I ll ask to make realize another film on the apollo 15 and 17 flyover, you'll be able to compare.>>*

After some great exclamations for the disclosure, "retiredafb" writes:

> <<*About But this particular mission brought to earth new tech and bio artefacts.*
>
> *The skies of Germany in 1945, saw the first "mama ships" coming in the*

---

65 For more information on Kent and his project, read at the link: http://www.cyberspaceorbit.com/

middle of the boxes. B17' cameras made good shots of them. Later, the R/D department of the pentagon transferred technologies to Bell laboratories, DuPont de Nemours and others. A lot of retired persons like me , write, publish. These things can seem ridiculous, like a man walking on the moon in 2007, but it was our job.>>

And in the following message posted, he says:

<<Most of the people now have no technical culture. I'm not surprised that people claim that mankind didn't go to the moon. Pictures of men walking on the moon are pictures who come from the future (for the youngest generations) and from the past. The illusion of progress associated with time...

The Apollo tapes show that it was possible better things, with ambition and ingeniosity. For me the most beautiful heritage of Apollo are pictures from the earth.>>

The last two messages posted, show all the Rutledge's disappointment, because of some nasty comments he received:

<<I refuse to answer to any revisionist comment , the same type of comment that can be found on the "apollo hoax subjects". About apollo 20 cancellation, consider that nasa claimed that the lm-15 was destructed . A billion dollar LM put to scrap? I'm amazed how lie become truth when printed on a wikipedia page. I would like to have the proof of intelligence lifeform on earth sometimes.

I'm not active on newsgroups, i just put references sometimes, i read them a lot, but i'm sick of that.>>

<<hello to all viewers, i answer to everybody by mail. I didn't want to post here but;

I live in Rwanda since 1994. The government provides me protection and discrecy, but digitizing and video treatment is poor here, so, don't be offended.The crew patch video made 90mb the first time, the team here didn't knew what a codec was, so only 4seconds 90mb 758-576 was posted. Same problems with subtitles, choice of a codec, format.>>[66]

---

66 Reproduction by kind permission. http://www.cyberspaceorbit.com/retiredafb.html

Other small details which show Rutledge's deep knowledge of Apollo program procedures and history

In my interview with "retiredafb", the alleged Apollo 20 Commander, said: <<I was located on the left window>> (see his answer to my question nr. 21, chapter I), regarding his position inside the Lunar Module. Well, I have found on the essay written by Scott and Leonov a small detail which confirms the information: the Commander of the mission occupied the left station inside the LEM (no seats for LEM, on the contrary of the Command Module).[67]

A. Leonov has always been indicated by "retiredafb" as LMP, the Lunar Module Pilot of the LM-15 Phoenix (Apollo 20), and as the matter of fact the LMP for Apollo missions occupied the right station in LM.

How can a simple hoaxer and joker know so many small details of space flight and space history, well included and connected in such a big context of history and reality? Of course it is possible for an actor, a joker, but after a long study and research, and it would be difficult. And even in that case, why spreading so many contradictions and silly mistakes in the context, after such a hard work of research? Spoiling everything in order to what?

But let us have a look to what he said about deserving test and fighter pilots, chosen to become astronauts in United States: in his answer to my question number 3, he wrote: <<[...] USAF uses every person who can bring skills, white, black, woman, every citizen. It was different with NASA, all astronauts were West Point students, only Alan Bean was an artist, Armstrong was a philosopher and Aldrin a spiritual man>>.

Not all the first NASA astronauts were West Point graduates, but many of them yes. And about the criteria of selection, I have found a confirmation of what Rutledge claimed, reading an old essay written by the famous journalist Italian Oriana Fallaci (Florence, 1929-2006): in her old reportage written for Italian magazines, and for her book *Se il sole muore* (in English means "If the sun dies"), she recollects her visit at NASA, during the 1960s, before the first landing on the Moon. She had the opportunity to interview eight NASA astronauts, and even dr. Wernher von Braun, who granted an astonishing interview.

---

67 *Glossary,* pages 399-400, *Two Sides of the Moon. Our Story of the Cold War Space Race,* by David Scott and Alexei Leonov, with Christine Toomey, Thomas Dunne Books, St. Martin's Press, First U.S. Edition, October 2004.

Oriana Fallaci asked herself and to her interlocutor why at the time NASA did not have as astronauts neither African-Americans nor women.

Donald K. Slayton ("Deke" for friends and fellows) was one of the first important people she met and interviewed. Slayton was the astronauts chief, at NASA: the head of the Astronaut Office[68]. With Oriana Fallaci he talked about the selection criteria used at the time, and about the NASA policy to select them and trained them. The Soviets had another policy, more concentrated on the automatic spacecrafts, rather than choosing good pilots, Slayton told her.

According to Slayton for NASA it was important - to become astronauts - being test pilots (with thousands of hours of flight) and technicians, for example. But D. Slayton told her they did not discriminate anybody, it did not matter what colour of the skin they had, and the fact to be man or woman. Only *"i meriti e basta"*[69], were important, he said in the Italian translation, which I can translate into English like: only merits, the values, and stop. Nothing else.

If you remember, William Rutledge said he was a test pilot; and the USAF - we can say now, notwithstanding Slayton's words, that NASA did not do that, at the beginning - selected African-Americans as astronauts, like Major Robert H. Lawrence, mentioned in chapter XII. But only him?

Well, if the William Rutledge testimony is true, or contains kernels of truth, we know now that a few years after Fallaci's interviews taken place in Houston and at Cape Kennedy, USAF had a woman astronaut, who was also an African-American astronaut: Stephanie Ellis (Abidjan, Ivory Coast, 1946-1975, USA?), chosen for her skills, but by secrecy (see my interview with William Rutledge).

With regard to Rutledge's statement on Buzz Aldrin, as "a spiritual man", it is very interesting what Aldrin said on TV in July 2009 (two years after my interview with William Rutledge); his opinion expressed on TV, was telecasted by C-SPAN. Aldrin reminded the general public

---

68 Slayton - officer with the USAF - resigned from the Air Force to become a full time NASA employee. He was promoted from head of Astronaut Office, to be Assistant Director of the Manned Spacecraft Center for Flight Crew Operations. A sort of Godfather for all astronaut, E. Cernan recollects in his memoirs (pag. 67, ibidem).

69 Chapter VIII, pag. 107. *Se il sole muore*, by Oriana Fallaci, Rizzoli, 1965, 21st edition, July 1981, Milan, Italy.

a feature of the Martian moon called Phobos: its monolith, an unusual structure visible on its surface. <<*There is a monolith [...] a very unusual structure on this little potato-shaped object that goes around Mars*>>, he said.

"Who put it there?", he asked to himself more than one time. His statements were discussed by several media networks.

So, who put it there? Aldrin answered: <<*The Universe. If you choose, God put it there.*>>

A remarkable statement pronounced by the former NASA astronaut, which is in accordance with the description made by William Rutledge, about the spirituality of this retired Colonel: Edwin E. "Buzz" Aldrin, Jr. (pilot for Gemini 12 and Apollo 11).

My point of view on contradictions and fakes of the disclosure: cryptic messages to NASA astronauts and to the public

Now the reader should have many references and coordinates to have a better opinion of the case. I suppose – it is my own working hypothesis on this aspect – that some of the contradictions of the case (like the video fake of the so-called "City", and the pollution with audio from previous Apollo missions, like Apollo 11, 15, 17) had the goal to send a message, both to the general public and to former NASA astronauts, like David Scott (educated at West Point), and whose voice is recognizable in the video of the "City": the video is a fake, but with audio coming from the Apollo 15 mission (see chapter III), and background made through photos taken by the Apollo 17 crew.

And David Scott is mentioned by "moonwalker1966delta" in my interview with him (year 2008). Scott would have met in 1993, in San Antonio, not only "moonwalker1966delta", but also Leonov and William Rutledge, the first deep throat of the case. By the way, Leonov in his biography *Two Sides of the Moon* writes that he regrets he was not able to go the Moon[70]. Does he mean that he was not able just with the Soviets[71], or not able to go in any case?

Colonel David Scott is as one of the astronauts well informed about

---

70 Pag. 376, chapter *Epilogue. 1975-2003*, of the book *Two Sides of the Moon*, by D. Scott and A. Leonov. The Soviets lost the space race with the U.S, above all, because of the failure of their rocket N-1.

71 A. Leonov was chosen by the Soviet Program as moonwalker for the Soviet Union.

previous Apollo missions, and especially about some USAF space missions, as I have already discussed it before.

Thus, it is likely that the video fake of the "City" was made to give less credibility to the case, but at the same time to send a cryptic message to David Scott himself, and providing a clue for the attentive public, about who could be one of the missing names of Apollo astronauts involved in Apollo 19 and 20 black operations, as crew members.

Another possible sign of this my hypothesis, could be the pollution of Apollo 20 footage, with Apollo 11 audio and footage. And, as the matter of fact, Neil Armstrong and Buzz Aldrin are indicated by "moonwalker1966delta" as backup crew members of Apollo 19, after the prime crew (Swigert, Ellis and Sorokin) was dismissed.

It meas that William Rutledge used since the beginning a code language, and only after some years, this could be enough comprehensible, on condition that we read the all story told us, beyond the simple opposition true-false. A disclosure with code messages.

The fact that there is a video fake made by photos coming from Apollo 17 archive, is in accordance with my hypothesis: with regard to this, there is the video <<*Apollo 17 ALIEN ENCOUNTER*>>[72], uploaded by "moonwalker1966delta" on November 20, 2009.

About this, a YouTube user asked the second deep throat to give some explanations: "mikevlove" asked him if the Apollo 17 crew visited the alien base located near their landing, if the base was active, and if the video were related to the alien depicted in the other video.

The answer by "moonwalker1966delta" - as YouTube comment – has been:

> <<*Yes, the base seemed active and the alien in the video was probably coming from that base. Anyway Apollo 17's crew haven't visited the base because they were not equipped for this. They only photographed and marked the base for future missions.*>>

This could explain the video uploaded by him the day before: November 19, 2009, and entitled <<*APOLLO 20 ALIEN MOONBASE*>>. The comment by "moonwalker1966delta" is: <<*View of an alien moonbase*

---

72 About the mistake he made mentioning Evans as one of LEM crew members (it is not possible), read the my observations, in the appendix

156

marked by Apollo 17 crew and filmed by Apollo 20 passing over Taurus Litthrow[73] before landing.Rutledge's and Leonov's voices.Original audio.>>

It seems to me there is a hidden strategy chosen by William Rutledge: not only the astronauts Aldrin and Armstrong, but even Eugene A. Cernan and Harrison H. Schmitt (Apollo 17), should know something about lunar anomalies and about space missions related to them.

We have always had the right clues under our eyes, in my opinion: William Rutledge ("retiredafb") had mentioned both Cernan and Schmitt, when on July 1st, 2007 he wrote to me a message with information as evidence of his identity and former career as astronaut:

<<[...]*The american flag used during apollo 17 , was the backup flag of the apollo 11 crew. Aldrin and Amstrong used it on the ground, in the KSC building during EVA training. This same flag is now on the ground of the moon, stucked near the steno crater. This old apollo 11 flag is in Taurus Littrow site, Gene Cernan or Harrisson Schmitt can confirm that, or Nasa maybe, but it is a detail omitted in space history.>>*

It was something I asked him as evidence of his identity as insider. At the time I did not think too much about these names. Why did he mention just Cernan and Schmitt? Now we have a possible answer.

If you - patient reader of this book - do not remember this passage, I invite you to read again the chapter V: <<*The Apollo 20 Case:Debunking or a Trojan Horse for the Truth?*>>

---

73 Usually written without the letter "h": Taurus-Littrow, not Taurus-Litthrow.

"Orange Mission": a Coloured Mission? The Secret DoD Program to investigate lunar anomalies

In one of latest videos posted on November 20, 2009, by "moonwalker1966delta" - the footage <<*APOLLO 20 EVA 3 EXTERNAL VIEW OF THE TRIANGULAR SHAPED SPACECRAFT*>> - there is a remarkable introduction, as subtitle. After the well-known Apollo 20 mission patch, there is a classification marking which says:

"ORANGE MISSION NASA-DoD-S-95-7024"

What does it mean? We can deduce – as pointed out many times by the insiders – that Pentagon and NASA have been working together on classified space missions, since long time ago. We already knew about that. But now we have one more clue: the expression "Orange Mission".

According to a source of information of mine (F.J.S.C.), in Spain – during the first or the second *Worldwide Symposium on Conspiracy Theory*[74] - there was a lecture with a presumed NASA footage, shown to the public. My source does not remember the name of the lecturer who presented the footage. For those interested, they could find it on YouTube, searching for <<*Constructions in the moon, Real secret footage*>>, uploaded by the YouTube user "AntenaParanoicaArc", in April 2009. The footage – which looks like a film taken during a flyover of a spacecraft, over the lunar surface – has an introduction with the same expression: "orange mission". Here the writing visible in a frame:

ORANGE MISSION

ZONE OF INTEREST

NASA-S-67-6938

Always according to another source (one of two insiders in contact with me and that I have interviewed), the Department of Defense had space missions called "Coloured Missions" (CM), developed after the ultra-secret space mission called "Apollo11-Apollo-D". I have no idea what "Apollo11-Apollo-D" were, but it seems another space mission launched by secrecy to the Moon, probably at the time of Apollo 11. Whatever the "Coloured Missions" could have been, it is interesting noticing that during the Apollo 17 mission, the geologist and astronaut

---

74 Spectra 09 was the second Worldwide Symposium on Conspiracy Theory, in València, 2-4 April 2009, was organized by Octubre Centre de Cultura Contemporània & Mess/Age. I was not able to find information on the first Worldwide Symposium. I suppose was Spectra 08, but I am not sure.

Harrison Schmitt found on the Moon the so-called "orange soil", one of the "most surprising discoveries" made by the Apollo program, Eugen Cernan writes in his memoirs *The Last Man on the Moon*.[75]

Conclusion

Of course I do not pretend to write the end for the Apollo 19 and 20 disclosure: a controversial case, an enigma. The strategy chosen by William Rutledge (he is allowed to speak out by the permission of some Government levels, probably) was communicate with the Internet public: users of files sharing communities and simple Internet citizens, providing footages polluted with images and audio from previous missions. The language? A strange English form, full of mistakes and grammatical slips, but at the same time the deep throat has provided detailed explanations of some Apollo program aspects, and presumed unknown historical episodes.

On the contrary, "moonwalker1966delta" has come forward with other footages, very technical and apparently boring; since my interview taken place with him (Sept-Oct 2008), he has been correcting the testimony by William Rutledge.

Step by step - through me and other YouTube users - "moonwalker1966delta" has increased the amount of information on the Apollo 19 and 20 case. Now the pieces of the puzzle are closer to each other, in spit of some of them are still missing, and some do not fit.

It seems the Apollo Soyuz Test Project was born thanks an idea by Philip Handler[76], former President of the U.S. National Academy of Sciences. At the cinema, in 1969, Dr. Handler saw the movie *Marooned*, directed by John Sturges (Columbia Pictures), a wonderful film with Gregory Peck, Richard Crenna and Gene Hackman, based on the novel by Martin Caidin.

---

75 Pages 332-334, Chapter 30, *Down in the Valley*, from the book *The Last Man on the Moon*, by E. Cernan and Don Davis, ibidem.

76 Consult the article by Livio Caputo entitled <<*Il compromesso spaziale*>>, July 1975, Italian magazine of the time (probably the weekly magazine *Epoca*, published in Italy until the end of the 1990s). L. Caputo (1933), was a correspondent for Italy, in USA. Dr. Philip Handler (1917-1981) was the eighteenth President of US National Academy of Sciences, from 1969 to 1981. Consult the essay *Philip Handler. A Biographical Memoir*, by Emil L. Smith and Robert L. Hill, National Academy of Sciences, 1985, Washington, D.C.

It was this movie to inspire him. Since that time, dr. Handler tried to convince Moscow and Washington of the importance to have spacecrafts capable of docking, in spite of different nationality and political belief of their crews (at the time, of course, Soviets and Americans developed different spacecrafts, and not conceived for an international cooperation in Space; it was the time of the Cold War). But was just that the main reason for the ASTP?

Maybe, one day other individuals will solve the mystery of the cigar-shaped-object, of other lunar anomalies, and of the presumed secret missions sent to the dark side of the Moon. Or maybe in the next future there will be either an official NASA press release, or an official declaration by another Agency of the U.S. Government: we are not alone in the Universe, because there are ruins of ancient alien civilizations, and derelict spacecrafts on the far side of the Moon.

In this case probably we have already evidence of that. The Apollo 19 and 20 crew members - and all the military and scientific staff involved in those classified mission and others – could be the testimonies of one of the most unbelievable, difficult and dangerous enterprise that humankind has ever achieved.

THE SECRET APOLLO 19 AND 20: PRIME AND BACKUP CREWS

Members of Apollo 19 original crew, dismissed about three weeks before launch, according to "moonwalker1966delta":

Stephanie ELLIS (1946-1975)

Alexei Vasiliyevich SOROKIN (1931-1976)

John L. SWIGERT, Jr. (1931-1982)

and members of Apollo 19 backup crew, who became the new crew for Apollo 19 mission:

"moonwalker1966delta", as CDR (who was also a Gemini astronaut),

another official Apollo program astronaut as pilot

another Russian cosmonaut "with exceptional medical skills"[77]

So the members of Apollo 19 backup crew became the main crew after the dismissal of the first crew. The insider nicknamed "moonwalker1966delta" (YouTube user) claims to be a former NASA astronaut (he has also been one of Gemini astronauts) and the Apollo 19 Commander of that new crew. According to his testimony, the new backup crew of Apollo 19 - which, at the Kennedy Space Center connected to Houston, helped on radio the fellow astronauts after their incident in Space occurred in February 1976 - was composed by at least two other NASA astronauts, whose names I disclose for the first time in this book:

Neil ARMSTRONG

Buzz ALDRIN

? (the third member)

---

77 Could he be Yuri V. Romanenko (born in 1944, USSR)? Neither confirmed nor denied by "moonwalker1966delta".

They would have worked inside the simulator at the KSC[78], during the incident. I do not know the name of the third member of the new backup crew.[79]

Always according to my sources of information, members of the Apollo 20 crew - launched to the dark side of the Moon in August 1976 - would have been:

Alexei LEONOV (LMP)

Leona Marietta SNYDER (CMP)

William RUTLEDGE (CDR)

---

78 For the reader, see the answer by "moonwalker1966delta" to my question nr. 2 of my interview with him: <<*Mission control for USA was in Vandenberg AFB but we have been forced to use Houston mission control for contingency situation due to incident occurred because the simulator Armstrong and Aldrin used was located at KSC and telemetry link data of the simulator was directly connected to Houston mission control as in usual Apollo Missions. That's why from that moment we used radio and data link with Houston mission control only.*>>, chapter VIII.

79 Of course the names of Armstrong and Aldrin come from a disclosure of an insider. I have written by e-mail to Buzz Aldrin in January 2010 to have a comment by him on this statement and his presumed involvement, but I did not get any answer so far (at the date of this publication). May I consider his silence as a "no comment" answer ? It is just a possibility.

THE VIDEOS POSTED ON YOUTUBE BY "RETIREDAFB"

The videos uploaded by "retiredafb" on YouTube from April until June 2007

Here you have a list of retiredafb's videos and comments posted on YouTube years ago, and later removed by retiredafb himself. The texts are presented without any correction, in their original form to the best of my knowledge (fortunately I saved them before they disappeared). It is possible that some of the video titles were a little different in their form (capital and small letters); the Web links are not completed.

APOLLO 20 legacy part 1 The CITY

duration (min. and seconds): 07'53"

posted on April 1, 2007

apollo 20, august 1976 mission went to the Delporte-Izsak part of the moon. CC was charles peter conrad, audio is unfortunately missing...

Despite the classified files, the apollo 20 belongs to all mankind It is a part of all human's heritage. Among the treasures found during the mission; the city, the spacecraft, the EBE mona lisa. Depending on the interest of viewers, i'll post 22 hours of tv transmissions from moon. Proofs that we are not alone, if there is still necessity to proove it. Nasa and USAF will be forced to tell the whole story before september 2007. If i do not post these files now, i'll never do it. This first part is an extract of the lunar rover transmission at mission elapsed time 140 , around iszak D, showing the city.

Those who want to have the definitive opinion, verify the possibility of hoax can verify on the nasa server , search as15 - 9625 and as15-9630 pictures who show the spaceship, subject of a future post.

http://www.lpi.usra.edu/resources/apo...

Please spread the word , the link on newsgroups, i don't know the list of groups interested by this subject

APOLLO 20 Legacy part 2 Crew patch

duration: 00'04"

posted on April 4, 2007

> End of Military conference 9 12 pm Vandenberg AFB Crew presentation and patch. CDR LMP and CMP

> "carpent tua poma nepotes"

ALIEN SPACESHIP ON THE MOON preflight study for APOLLO 20

duration: 00'56"

posted on April 5, 2007

> Anaglyphic study preflight of Apollo 20. Assembly of the two frames seen by Apollo 15 AS15-9625 and AS15-9630.

> Check my videos, Apollo 20 movies of the spaceship and the pilot will be posted soon.

> Warning: not a hoax, some of these pictures and movies can be seen on the offical sites of the NASA.

> http://www.lpi.usra.edu/resources/apo...

> "carpent tua poma nepotes"

APOLLO 20 legacy part 1 The City

duration: 05'02"

posted on April 7, 2007

> Sound version of the 1st video; other codec.apollo 20, august 1976 mission went to the Delporte-Izsak part of the moon.

> Despite the classified files, the apollo 20 belongs to all mankind It is a part of all human's heritage. Among the treasures found during the mission; the city, the spacecraft, the EBE mona lisa. Depending on the interest of viewers, i'll post 22 hours of tv transmissions from moon. Nasa and USAF will be forced to tell the whole story before september 2007. This first part is an extract of the lunar rover transmission at mission elapsed time 140 , around iszak D, showing the city.

> Those who want to have the definitive opinion, verify the possibility

of hoax can verify on the nasa server , search as15 - 9625 and as15 9630 pictures who show the spaceship, subject of a future post.

http://www.lpi.usra.edu/resources/apo...

Please spread the word , the link on newsgroups, i don't know the list of groups interessed by this subject.

APOLLO 20 Legacy liftoff of Apollo 20 saturne 5

duration: 00'36"

posted on April 9, 2007

Lift off of Apollo 20 saturn 5 from Vandenberg AFB august 16 1976. Note the marks on the rocket, different than the previous apollo launches.

"carpent tua poma nepotes"

check my account, the big apollo 20 files wil be posted soon, especially the most important

ALIEN SPACESHIP ON THE MOON stills from APOLLO 20

duration: 01'52"

posted on May 3, 2007

3 stills metric photography made by alexei leonov during the last revolution before descent on the Izsak Y Crater. More details visible than the apollo 15 panoramic shot.

(http://www.lpi.usra.edu/resources/apo...)

Check also the flyover TV feed during this revolution

ALIEN SPACESHIP ON THE MOON flyover bef. landing APOLLO 20

duration: 05'53''

posted on May 4, 2007

> TV Feed from the lunar module LM-15 during the last revolution before descent. LM passes over Tsiolkovski, Fermi, Delporte and Lukte before passing on the Izsak Y crater. The spaceship is filmed with close telephoto lens, revealing more details. CDR communicates the South -East coordinates of the major parts of the spaceship, approximately 4 kilometers long. Color distortions are caused by the rotating wheel inside the Westinghouse Color TV Camera.

APOLLO 15 and 17 search for the spaceship

duration: 00'37''

posted on May 6, 2007

> Apollo 15 made the discovery CDR scott did these shots. Apollo 17 made the shots preparing the landing site choice. These pictures can be found on the official nasa apollo atlas at
>
> http://www.lpi.usra.edu/resources/apollo/catalog/metric/

One of Nasa attempt to hide Alien Spacecraft

duration: 00'35''

posted on May 11, 2007

> In the late 70's, nasa tried to hide alien artifacts. When you try to download this Apollo 17 spacecraft picture, you get a complete low-res photography:
>
> http://www.lpi.usra.edu/resources/apo...
>
> If you want to get the hires print photography, you get this one:
>
> http://www.lpi.usra.edu/resources/apo...
>
> Apollo 15 used 4*5 inches silver negatives. No flight problem or scanner distorsion can justify such a mess. A natural negative problem is this one; end of a magazin.
>
> http://www.lpi.usra.edu/resources/apo...
>
> In late 70's nasa couldn't anticipate public internet ,so , it's a nice bad

168

disinformation attempt.

APOLLO 20 Test EVA 1

duration: 00'23"

posted on June 18, 2007:

>Test mpeg compressor. Lyosha near rosetta stone at station 1 EVA 1

APOLLO 20 Test Launch Pad

duration: 00'31"

posted on June 18, 2009

>Test WMV compressor . Launch pad July 15.

APOLLO 20 TEST Snyder Ingress

duration: 00'33"

posted on June 18, 2009

>Test Cinepak radius compressor. Rutledge and L. Marietta Snyder ingress

APOLLO 20 ALIEN SPACESHIP ON THE MOON CSM FLYOVER

duration: 02'18"

posted on June 24, 2009

>CSM 16 mm footage through the AGC lens, made by Leona Snyder [...][80] lunar orbit revolutions. Camera is fixed on the eyepiece of the telescope, less dropouts or moves than the Tv feed from the LM. Frame transfer is not perfect, speed is faster than actual, 4 different speeds were used on the 16 mm camera. The landing site is visible on the lower part in the first lunar sequence

>sorry for the first viewers and commenters, i had to upload again with a better codec

---

80   Not comprehensible. That's why I have put the dots.

The new videos uploaded on YouTube in January 2008

In January 2008, William Rutledge ("retiredafb" on YouTube) posted other two videos, apparently unpublished, about the lost crew of STS-107 (the incident in space occurred in 2003). After a few days the videos were removed by "retiredafb" himself.

NASA SECRET TAPES – STS 107 – part 1 Apollo 20

duration: 06'40"

posted on January 4, 2008

> Secret because never broadcasted before or avaiable since 2003 on any nasa site.
>
> For those who believe that space programs are opened. Inflight tapes just after the wake up calls. A tribute to the astronauts. Part 1

NASA SECRET TAPES – STS 107 – part 2 Apollo 20

duration: 09'17"

posted on January 4, 2008

> For those who believe that space programs are opened. Secret because not avaiable since 2003 on any nasa site. Inflight tapes just after the wake up calls.
>
> A tribute to the astronauts. Part 2

The last video uploaded on YouTube by "retiredafb"

After to have removed all his videos, apparently "retiredafb" decided to continue his disclosure on another community of files sharing: revver.com.[81] But before to do that, in April 2008 he added on YouTube a new video, like a trailer of his leak of information, with his new address for those interested in his testimony. Very meaningful the sound-track chosen by him: it is *Mars, the Bringer of War*, the beginning of the orchestral piece *The Planets* (performed in 1918-20), by Gustav Holst, a British composer (1874-1934) who was interested in theosophy.

APOLLO 20 new videos new adress

posted on April 9, 2008

duration: 01'30"

APOLLO 20 new videos uploaded, new adress for future posts

In the footage we can read that <<*all new videos are posted on www.revver.com/u/retiredafb*>> But it is more interesting – perhaps - the new profile he has edited on YouTube: here you have the transcription of the text:

> <<*I have too many problems with youtube who never answer my questions, the new videos will be online an another site www.revver.com, they are already there, and the new ones , the most important soon.*
>
> *My account and messages, have been spoofed many weeks ago. Some messages have been fakened, my messages send since august are not written by my hand. Thoses messages included the special linguistic marks i placed usually. Some people oppened accounts using my name, tried to spoof email boxes, closed some videos, send invitationson youtube etc... To those who did the job; congratulations, you are well paid .*
>
> *I closed my two rwandacell Mtn numbers. I'll open a site in cocoa island and put some other new videos here. I'm searching an old 2 inches video player to grab the eva sounds.*>>[82]

---

81 Consult the website: http://www.gustavholst.info/

82 http://www.youtube.com/user/retiredafb

TRANSCRIPTION OF THE PRESUMED RADIO DIALOGUE
AMONG MISSION CONTROL IN VANDENBERG
AND THE LEM PHOENIX (LM-15)

ALIEN SPACESHIP ON THE MOON flyover bef. landing APOLLO 20

Video Added: May 04, 2007

From: retiredafb

> TV Feed from the lunar module LM-15 during the last revolution before descent. LM passes over Tsiolkovski, Fermi, Delporte and Lukte before passing on the Izsak Y crater. The spaceship is filmed with close telephoto lens, revealing more details. CDR communicates the South -East coordinates of the major parts of the spaceship, approximately 4 kilometers long. Color distortions are caused by the rotating wheel inside the Westinghouse Color TV Camera.

Transcription of the video subtitles by Luca Scantamburlo (without any correction, in spite of mistakes and the unusual English form).

- 00:10   *Vandenberg Twenty Tiros are good sound is one five*

- 00.15   *Twenty Vandenberg sound is two five*

- 00:19   *Vandenberg Twenty, i fix the cam...*

           on the... bar

- 00:27   *Vandenberg Twenty We passed over Tsiolkovsky*

           and we are over Fermi now

- 00:37   *Vandenberg twenty Delporte is visible with it's*

           Y shaped central peak

- 00:51   *and below os Lutke*

           on the [not comprehensible] *lower side*

- 00:56   *Izsak whould be visible behind the lem thrusters, for a*
           few seconds

- 01:44   *Izsak is visible on the upper left side of the*
           window, [three words not comprehensible] *off the T bar the*

- 02:57   *Twenty Vandenberg, set the aperture to*
           one point eight

- 03:03   *Vandenberg Twenty, roger i'm focusing*
           on telephoto lens now

- 03:12   *Twenty Vandenberg, which is the magazin used*
           one point eight

- 03:18   *Vandenberg Twenty, alexei is taking some metric shots*
           with the hasselblad frame count is 1019

- 03:24   *Vandenberg Twenty, we have a fantastic view over*
           the ship the lens are stuck on the window i hope you

- 03:34   *Vandenberg Twenty, i'm ready to transmit the marks*
           for the CSM DSKY

- 03:43   *GO*

- 04:13   *Vandenberg Twenty, nose is one seven point three South*
           one one seven point six two East

- 04:25   *cockpit is one seven point two five South*
           one one seven point six two East

- 04:36   *the base is one seven point two zero South*
           one one seven point six two East
           and the base is burried

- 04:50   *we can see meteor impacts on the body*
           the surface is crusted and covered with some dust
           it's huge

- 05:05   *in the shdow below the ship we can see somthing*
          like a landing gear......three parts...barrels

- 05:14   *on the landing site, there are many pieces*
          of metal, shiny parts look like gold or mylar

- 05:27   *the ship is in bad condition is must be here....*
          Billions of years

- 05:33   *..........."landing site"...........*

- 05:49   *Vandenberg Twenty the ship will be out of view*
          it should be hidden behins the porch

APPENDIX IV

THE VIDEOS POSTED ON YOUTUBE BY
"MOONWALKER1966DELTA"

"moonwalker1966delta" - the alleged Apollo 19 Commander - is a YouTube user since August 30, 2007. Here you have the list of the videos (with their comments) he has uploaded on his YouTube channel so far (at the date of December 2009). No corrections brought in the text.

Apollo 20 Snyder ingress

duration: 34"

posted on September 14, 2007

> Leona Snyder and Leonov entering Apollo 20 CSM

Apollo 20 mixed footage

duration: 1' 01"

posted on January 18, 2008

> 3 different views of Apollo 20 mission's LEM from top of a hill,close view and unknown view of part of the LEM

Apollo 20 preparing for DPI

duration: 01' 57"

posted on February 12, 2008

> Shots by Leonov during phase of preparing for DPI.Sunrise on the Moon.Original sound with W.Rutledge's voice talking to
>
> Vandemberg Mission Control

Apollo 20 EVA1

duration: 01' 23"

posted on February 25, 2008

> During EVA 1 W.Rutledge communicates to Houston about a problem on Phoenix's hatch.Voice from Leonov too.Communications are all by Tyros satellite

Apollo 19 incident

duration 01' 21"

posted on November 09, 2008

> Apollo 19 just hit by something and loosing telemetry data.Fire and smoke on AC-BC cell bus and aborting mission after TLI insertion

APOLLO20 EVA2 ON THE WAY TO THE MOTHERSIP[83]

duration: 02' 31"

posted on July 4, 2009

> No audio because encrypted and transmitted separately

APOLLO 20 ALIEN MOONBASE

duration: 00' 36"

posted on November 19, 2009

> View of an alien moonbase marked by Apollo 17 crew and filmed by Apollo 20 passing over Taurus Litthrow before landing.Rutledge's and Leonov's voices.Original audio.

---

83 Notice the missing"h" in the word.

APOLLO 17 ALIEN ENCOUNTER

duration: 00' 37"

posted on November 20, 2009

> Proof of encounter between Apollo 17 Crew and an alien of the near base. In this video it is possible to see Commander Cernan to run towardspilot Evans[84] who was not awarned[85] of the stranger's presence and to push him towards the Lem.Cernan's stressed voice is askin Evans and Mission Control to change to Primary Channel used for all Apollo Missions to talk about strange or alien encounters on the moon.

APOLLO 20 EVA 3 EXTERNAL VIEW OF THE TRIANGULAR SHAPED SPACECRAFT

duration: 01' 21"

posted on November 20, 2009

> External view of the triangular shaped spacecraft.Audio encrypted.

---

84 This is not possible (Evans on the lunar surface). According to the official Space history – and according to Eugene Cernan's book, *The Last Man on the Moon*, written with Don Davis – the LEM crew of Apollo 17 was composed by Harrison H. (Jack) Schmitt (as LMP) and Eugene A. Cernan (as Apollo 17 CDR). Ronald E. Evans was the CMP, in parking orbit around the Moon. An Italian friend of mine – Mr. Valerio U. - contacted "moonwalker1966delta" at the end of 2009 by YouTube/General Messages, and asked him about this inconsistency, and he got the answer that it is a mistake he made. Because even Ronald Evans would have had a close encounter in Space. Did he mean his EVA (extravehicular activity) during the trans-earth coast phase of the return flight, as the biographical data of Johnson Space Center said? So, we can consider that mistake like a lapsus calami, or a mistake made on purpose to tell us something else. My opinion is he made this silly mistake on purpose, either to give less credibility to its disclosure, or to tell us something else. It seems a nonsense, but considering the rumors of the so-called Public Acclimation Program, it has its logic. Unfortunately R. Evans – who was also a USN Captain and the backup CMP for the Apollo-Soyuz Test Project mission– died of a heart attack in 1990, so we cannot ask him anything. But there was a "terrible spacewalk" for him – according to E. Cernan – to retrieve the film of the mission Apollo 17 outside the spacecraft America; see about it on pag. 340 of Cernan's book. Of course in the context of the book, there is not any close encounter at all. But it seems that "moonwalker1966delta" knew the anectode of this terrible spacewalk.

85 "awarned" is not correct. Maybe he meant "aware". This is a classical example of a series of mistakes that are frequent in this disclosure.

APOLLO 19 LAUNCH

duration: 00' 04"

posted on November 20, 2009

Vandeberg Air Force Base Complex 6 Apollo 19 launch. February the 2nd 1976 05.30 AM Western time.The only Apollo launch with a yellow tower and no NASA signs on the rocket as for Apollo 20

The Book by Rami: A Tribute for My Israeli Friend

Jan 2010, by Rami Bar Ilan – Artist, born in 1955 (Israel)

I attended the Ontario College of Art (OCA), in Toronto, Canada, in 1977/78 and the Sheridan College Classical Animation Department, Oakville, (Ontario) in 1983/84. But I consider myself a self-taught person.

In 1973 I served in IDF (Israeli Defense Forces) as a combat paratrooper with the 890th Battalion. During the Yom Kippur War my company was attached to General Ariel Sharon's Army for Special Operations. Our unit commander was Major Shmuel Arad, and we operated under 14th Armored Brigade, Commander Colonel Amnon Reshef.

Our unit participated in the greatest battles of Yom Kippur War in the Sinai desert and Egyptian property, including the second greatest tank battle in history since Kursk in WWII. Over 2000 tanks were engaged in this battle.

In 2001 I decided to write a book, to tell of the horror we lived through in this war, tell our story for posterity so that this terrible horror will not be forgotten. We served our country... did we not? I interviewed over 60 veterans of this war, troopers, officers and Commanders that served with me and finally wrote the book. It tool 420 pages and 7 years to complete. The book is called "Goodbye To Love".

In 2008 the General Censor, a high ranking IDF Officer that controls Israeli MOD Department, imposing military censorship authority on written publications under the Israeli Law, heard of my book and contacted me by phone, advising me to submit the manuscript for review by military censor and obtain permission for the publication. Otherwise I would have faced charges, probably. After to have reviewed the book, the General Censor rejected 26 parts of the text, and in one case a whole page. In my book I did not disclose any classified information or any military secret. The book deals strictly with the human aspect of war and the terrible burden indelibly stamped into the young minds of the unseasoned troopers by the seemingly senseless mass slaughter.

The Military Censor reasons for the rejections were: "Israeli-Egypt relations and misconduct of IDF troops..." My discussion with the Censor, resulted in canceling only a couple of minor restrictions. I was also told that the Law does not permit to black-mark the censored texts, so the reader could at least know what part of the story were censored. I was told to re-edit the fractured, mutilated texts, to make the story seamless, so that the reader will not notice the gaps. Then to submit the book again for the Censor review to qualify it for a publication.

I refused to do that. I think that this censorship may not even be legal. But the only option I have is to apply to the Supreme Court, which is not realistic at this time because the high cost of it is beyond my means. So there is an impasse and this is where things stand now. I am working to sort all this out somehow and hoping to publish my book with the full text in the future. Thank you for reading

Bless life, bless people, respect, appreciate

Rami Bar Ilan   www.ramistrip.com

APPENDIX VI

Lunar Maps and Photos

Features of the far side of the Moon: the black and big Tsiolkovsky crater with its bright peak – is visible at the center.

The Fermi walled Plane and the several Izsak craters, are visible on its left

Image credit: The Lunar and Planetary Institute – NASA Photo

LUNAR AND PLANETARY INSTITUTE

LEM-1A
LUNAR EARTHSIDE HEMISPHERE
USAF LUNAR REFERENCE MOSAIC
3RD EDITION JULY 1967

LUNAR LANDING SITE CHART
LEM-1A, Lunar Earthside hemisphere, USAF Lunar Reference Mosaic
3rd Edition, July 1967

Image credit: The Lunar and Planetary Institute

My Dedication

This book – as some of my Website pages – is dedicated to all astronauts and cosmonauts who lost their life in Space on duty under classified operations; to all astronauts and cosmonauts who are retired, sick, and they feel themselves close to death; to all women and men who have been to Space by secrecy and who believe that with their death an important piece of history will be lost forever. To the people who have been key-witnesses of unknown historical events whose knowledge could be crucial for the mankind's future.

If the YouTube users by the names of "retiredafb" (the alleged William Rutledge, Apollo 20 CMDR) and "moonwalker1966delta" (the alleged Apollo 19 CMDR) have decided to speak out – or they are allowed to speak out - perhaps it is because they are not currently employed by a Space agency (military or civilian) anymore and they believe that their disclosure will not cause any damage to their country and to National security, but on the contrary their revelation could help either to defeat a hidden threat which is a danger for their country and the world, or helping to widen mankind horizons in every dimension, both technological and spiritual...

As pointed out by William Rutledge in one of his comments on YouTube: <<[...] *the apollo 20 belongs to all mankind It is a part of all human's heritage*>>.

Virgilio wrote: <<*Carpent tua poma nepotes*>>. The Apollo 20 patch quotes it. Maybe we are those grandchildren...

L. Scantamburlo

To whom it may concern:

my e-mail: *info@angelismarriti.it*

www.angelismarriti.it

BIBLIOGRAPHY

Cosmo. Atlante dell'Universo. Istituto Geografico De Agostini, 1985, Novara (Italy). Original Title: *The Atlas of the Universe,* Mitchell Beazley Ltd, London, 1970-1981, UK; edited by Patrick Moore.

CERNAN Eugene and DAVIS Don, *The Last Man on the Moon,* St. Martin's Griffin, New York, USA, 1999, Tenth Anniversary Edition, June 2009.

CUNNINGHAM Walter, *I ragazzi della luna,* edited by Giovanni Caprara, Ugo Mursia Editore, Italian edition, Milan (Italy), 2009, translation by Umberto Cavallaro.

FALLACI Oriana, *Se il sole muore,* Rizzoli Editore, Milan, 1965, 21st Italian Edition, July 1981.

IRWIN James B., *More Than Earthlings,* Broadman Press, Nashville, Tennessee, USA, 1983.

KEITH Jim, *Casebook on Alternative 3: UFOs, Secret Societies and World Control,* IllumiNet Press, first edition, Lilburn, GA, USA, 1994.

LIGHT Michael, *Luna,* Italian edition, edited by Giovanni Caprara, Arnoldo Mondadori Editore, Milan, 1999, translation by Guido Lagomarsino (*Full Moon,* by M. Light, with the essay *The Farthest Place,* by Andrew Chaikin, Jonathan Cape, Random House, London, 1999).

MONTGOMERY, Scott L., *Luna. Segreti e misteri del nostro satellite,* Italian edition, translation from English into Italian by Daniele Ballarini, White Star, Vercelli, Italy, 2009. Weldon Owen Production, Sydney, Australia.

SERVIO Marzio, *Cum Grano Salis. Il latino per l'uomo di mondo,* A. Vallardi, Garzanti Editore, Milan, 1992, fourth edition, Feb. 1995.

SCOTT David and LEONOV Alexei, with Christine Toomey, *Two Sides of the Moon. Our Story of the Cold War Space Race.* Thomas Dunne Books, St. Martin's Press, First U.S. Edition, October 2004. First published in Great Britain by Simon & Schuster, A Viacom Company.

VIDEO DOCUMETARIES AND FILM

Apollo 11. L'uomo sulla Luna, a film by Steve Ruggi, Milan, 2009, Cinehollywood, Special Edition for the 40th Anniversary; Italian edition of *One Giant Leap: Moonlanding,* Discovery Channel, produced by George Carey, A Barraclough Carey Production for Discovery Networks and Channel Four Television.

Maaroned. Abbandonati nello spazio, by John Sturges, Columbia Pictures, 1969, renewed 1997, Columbia TriStar Home Entertainment, Italian edition, 2004, based on a novel by Martin Caidin.

TABLE AND ABBREVIATIONS

Inch: 2,54 cm

Astronomical Unit (U.A.): 149.597.870 km

Foot: 30,479 cm

Nautical Mile (knot) USA: 1,853 km

Terrestrial Mile: 1,61 km

AGC: Apollo Guidance Computer

ASTP: Apollo Soyuz Test Project

CAPCOM: Spacecraft Communicator

CDR/CMDR: Commander (left station in LM, and left seat in CM)

CM: Command Module

CMP: Command Module Pilot, the navigator (center seat in CM)

CSM: Command and Service Modules (the Apollo spacecraft)

DoD: Department of Defense

DSKY: Display Keyboard (Apollo Spacecraft)

EVA: Extravehicular activity, outside a spacecraft, in Space and on the ground (of satellites or planets)

JSC: Johnson Space Center (in Houston, named the MSC until 1973)

LM/LEM: Lunar Excursion Module

LYOSHA: nickname used, for example, by S. P. Korolev to address A. Leonov[86]

LPI: The Lunar and Planetary Institute (research institute in Houston)

LMP: Lunar Module Pilot (right station in LM, but left seat CSM)

MET: Mission Elapsed Time

NASA: National Aeronautics and Space Administration

TLI: Trans Lunar Injection, the maneuver used to set a spaceship into a translunar trajectory from Earth orbit

USAF: United States Air Force (U.S. Air Force)

---

86 It is very interesting that William Rutledge knew the nickname used with Leonov: you can find the reference in the memoirs by General A. Leonov, written with D. Scott: *Two Sides of the Moon*, pag. 111, Chapter 4, *A Fair Solar Wind*, ibidem. "retiredafb" used Lyosha in message to Luca Scantamburlo (YouTube Account/General Messages, June 24, 2007), and for a YouTube video comment: <<*APOLLO 20 Test EVA 1*>>, duration: 00'23", posted on June 18, 2007. See the Appendix II.

First Edition, January 2010

Lulu.com, USA, 2010

ISBN 978-1-4452-7397-6

Lightning Source UK Ltd.
Milton Keynes UK
UKOW051855220512

193100UK00001B/35/P